MAIN-COURSE SOUPS

RAY L. OVERTON

Photographs by Mark Hill

LONGSTREET PRESS
Atlanta, Georgia

This book is lovingly dedicated to my parents,
Jan and Ray Overton, who taught me by their
example about life and unconditional love.
And to my Granny Lou, who
continually inspires me
every day.

Published by
LONGSTREET PRESS, INC.
A subsidiary of Cox Newspapers,
A subsidiary of Cox Enterprises, Inc.
2140 Newmarket Parkway
Suite 122
Marietta, GA 30067

Printed in the United States of America
1st printing, 1997
Library of Congress Catalog Card Number: 97-73570
ISBN: 1-56352-445-7

Book and jacket design by Burtch Bennett Hunter

Contents

INTRODUCTION

I love soups, especially main-course soups. I love to order these soups when I eat out, but mostly I love to make them at home. Soup fills my kitchen with the sights, smells, and tastes I love most: aromatic stock bubbling on the stove; colorful vegetables ready for peeling, slicing, and sautéing; freshly chopped herbs perfuming the air. When the weather is inclement—and even when it's not—I find nothing more comforting than to surround myself with the familiar tasks of soup making.

I didn't appreciate soups as a child. In my family, soups were made for economic reasons, not for the pleasure they could bring. If they weren't made from whatever ingredients were hanging around the refrigerator or pantry, they were usually from a can. (My favorite was chicken and stars.) Happily, my childhood indifference did not last. Over many years of cooking and teaching cooking, I have developed a love affair with soups. The more sophisticated my tastes became, the more I craved the many flavors and textures that good soups provide.

Soups have a proven track record for those of us who entertain frequently. What other recipes in our culinary repertoire have so many advantages? With a fresh salad, crusty bread, and fruit or sorbet for dessert, a hearty soup can make a complete meal. Such a meal can easily and economically serve eight guests with only a pound or two of meat. What's more, soup can be made in the morning and then simmered slowly throughout the day, with only the occasional stir. Or it can be made completely ahead of time, frozen, and defrosted for impromptu gatherings. When your guests arrive, there is no last-minute push to get everything on the table. When I make soup, I enjoy it just as much the second or third day. The flavors have a chance to mingle, and the result is often more satisfying than the initial creation.

The soups in this book are the result of roughly five years of testing, tasting, and teaching. During this time I have learned some valuable guidelines for soup making that have helped to make my efforts much more rewarding. Here are a few tips to get you started.

Equipment
Stockpots and Dutch Ovens

The "batterie de cuisine," or kitchen arsenal, for soup making is quite simple. The main tool for beginning a soup is the **stockpot** or large, covered **casserole** or **Dutch oven**. You will need something that can comfortably hold five to eight quarts of liquid. I prefer a tall, heavy-gauge steel stockpot for making my stock and a cast-iron pot with an enameled finish for making the soup itself. Not only do both these types of pots clean well, but their material will not react with acidic ingredients such as wine, tomatoes, and citrus juices. Tight-fitting lids allow the soup to simmer without loss of liquid or flavor.

The ideal stockpot is twice as tall as it is wide, with sturdy handles on each side. The higher sides of the pot guard against too-rapid evaporation of liquid. The more narrow base allows for even heat distribution. A stock should always be simmered on as low a heat as possible, low enough that only tiny bubbles reach the surface of the stock. Slow simmering rather than boiling helps prevent the stock from becoming cloudy.

Deep, covered casseroles and Dutch ovens are the modern-day equivalents of the old-fashioned stew pots that hung in the fireplace hearth. These pots are an excellent choice for making the soups in this book. Also, because of their tight-fitting lids and heavy cast-iron material, they make wonderful vessels for braising or slow cooking other dishes, either in the oven or on the stovetop. It makes no difference whether the casserole or Dutch oven is round or oval. Many of these pots have a brightly colored enamel coating, which makes them beautiful enough to bring right from the stove to the table for serving.

When choosing your pot, keep in mind that weight is the most important characteristic for all stovetop cooking. The thinner and more lightweight the material, the greater the risk of scorching the food. It is very difficult to maintain a proper and constant dispersion of heat using lighter (and usually less expensive) pots. As I see it, your kitchen equipment should be regarded as an investment, one that will withstand the rigors of everyday cooking. Over time, an investment in a high-quality stockpot or Dutch oven will pay off because you will not have to replace cheaper equipment or discard food that has been ruined because of improper cookware.

My final thought on whether to use a stockpot, covered casserole, or Dutch oven is this: Use what you have, so long as it can easily accommodate all the ingredients in the soup. My goal is to get you to cook, enjoy, and share these recipes with the important people in your life.

Other Equipment

High on my list of soup-making equipment is a **food mill** or **food processor**, essential for pureeing soups into a smooth consistency. A food processor is also valuable for chopping the often large quantities of vegetables called for in soups. A heavy-duty **colander** or **wire mesh strainer** is needed for straining a soup's solids from its liquid before pureeing. **Cheesecloth** is good for sieving out smaller particles that the strainer cannot catch; line the strainer with a triple thickness of dampened cheesecloth. (If I want the ultimate in smooth texture, I will pour my pureed solids back through the strainer, pressing and forcing them through with the back of a wooden spoon or ladle.)

To round out the ideal equipment list, include the following items: a good-quality **cutting board** (I prefer a tough acrylic surface); a sturdy, well-balanced stainless-steel **chef's knife**; a smaller **paring knife** for peeling and cutting up smaller ingredients; one set each of liquid and dry **measuring cups**; a set of **measuring spoons**; a **wooden spoon** for stirring; a **spatula** for scraping the sides of the pot and processor; a **ladle** for serving; a **wire whisk** for smooth incorporations of cheeses, sour cream, and half and half; a swivel-style **vegetable peeler**; a **citrus zester** (ideal for removing the peel without the bitter white pith); and, finally, a **wire mesh skimmer** for removing any foam or scum from the surface of stocks and soups as they are cooking.

Stocks

As with anything you make, soups should contain the freshest ingredients available. That includes homemade stock. If you've never made stock, relax. It's easy. The main thing to remember is not to boil the stock. It should gently simmer. Rapid boiling produces a murky end result. After a stock reaches the initial boil, reduce the temperature, skim any scum from the top of the stock, and allow the stock to gently simmer for the allotted amount of time. Now, read on. I have a confession to make. . . .

I don't always have time to make a homemade stock, and when I don't, I have no qualms about using a canned broth. Do not let the absence of homemade stock prevent you from making soup! There are a number of canned broth varieties on the market. I look for those that are low in sodium. When a recipe calls for reducing the liquid in a soup, a broth high in sodium content will make the concentrated liquid too salty. Some cookbooks include recipes for canned broth "enhancers"—that is, recipes for simmering canned broth with a little onion, carrot, celery, and other vegetables that add flavor to the broth. Enhancers are not necessary when using the broth for soup, because it will simmer with additional ingredients anyway. Save this enhancer method for a rice pilaf, risotto, sauce, gravy, or any dish that will not have the benefit of slow simmering.

The four classic stocks described below—chicken, beef, fish, and vegetable—can all be made ahead and kept for two to three days refrigerated and up to two weeks frozen. I like to make stock on weekends when the weather is uncooperative. The beauty of stock is that once everything is in the pot, it can simmer for hours (with the exception of fish stock, which cooks for about 20 to 30 minutes). After cooking, strain the stock, chill for as little as 15 minutes and up to several hours or overnight, and remove the fat that has risen to the top. (I've always said if it was that easy for us to get rid of excess fat, you'd find me sleeping in the refrigerator. But that's another story.)

Nowadays you can find a kitchen gadget for just about anything. Fat-skimming ladles and strainers for separating fat from liquid (the latter look like measuring cups with a spout at the bottom) come in a variety of styles. None of these works as well for me as my refrigerator and a zip-top freezer bag. Here's my quick method for defatting chicken or beef stock: Strain the stock into a bowl and transfer it to a gallon-sized freezer bag. Place the sealed bag (in a bowl for support) in the refrigerator for about 10 to 15 minutes. Remove the bag from the refrigerator and hold it over a bowl. Using a pair of kitchen shears, carefully snip one corner from the bottom of the bag and allow the stock to drain into the bowl. When the stock has finished draining and the level in the bag is approaching the greasy layer of fat, pinch the bag tight to stop the flow. Fold the snipped corner closed, tape or staple it shut, and throw the bag away.

CLASSIC CHICKEN STOCK

A well-made chicken stock makes a big difference in assuring your soup's final flavor and ultimate success. I like to buy whole chickens and cut them up at home, reserving the wings, backs, and necks in a zip-top freezer bag until I have enough to make a delicious stock. Never add the chicken's liver to your stock; it will make the stock bitter and will cloud the finished result.

Makes 2 quarts

1 (3 TO 4 POUND) CHICKEN OR 3 TO 4 POUNDS CHICKEN
    WINGS, BACKS, NECKS, ETC.

3½ QUARTS WATER

2 ONIONS, QUARTERED (UNPEELED)

3 GARLIC CLOVES

1 CARROT, CUT IN HALF

1 RIB OF CELERY, CUT IN HALF

FRESH HERB BOUQUET OF 1 BAY LEAF, 2 SPRIGS OF THYME,
    AND 4 PARSLEY STALKS, TIED WITH KITCHEN TWINE

10 BLACK PEPPERCORNS

In a heavy 8-quart stockpot, combine all ingredients. Bring to a boil, reduce the heat to low, and carefully skim off any scum that rises to the top. Cover and simmer for 1 to 1½ hours.

Remove the chicken from the broth and set aside to cool. When the chicken is cool enough to handle, remove the meat from the bone and reserve the meat for another use. Return the bones to the stockpot and continue simmering, uncovered, for 2 hours.

Strain the stock and discard the solids. Allow the stock to cool to room temperature, then refrigerate for several hours or overnight. Carefully remove the layer of hardened fat from the surface. (Alternatively, use the quick method of defatting stock, page 3.) Stock will keep for 2 to 3 days refrigerated and for up to 2 months frozen. Defrost overnight in the refrigerator.

CLASSIC BEEF STOCK

By first roasting the bones and then the vegetables, you are guaranteed a rich-tasting, beautifully colored stock. Many larger supermarkets now sell beef bones (sometimes labeled for the family pet) at a nominal charge. Don't be concerned if the roasted bones and vegetables appear very dark. You want them to be charred around the edges, with lots of browned bits accumulating in the bottom of the roasting pan. Do not use a nonstick roasting pan, as this virtually eliminates the flavorful browned bits needed for the deglazing step in this recipe.

Makes 2 quarts

5 POUNDS BEEF OR VEAL BONES, SUCH AS NECKS, SHANKS, KNUCKLES, OR TAILS

3 ONIONS, QUARTERED (UNPEELED)

2 CARROTS, CUT IN HALF

2 RIBS OF CELERY, CUT IN HALF

3½ QUARTS WATER

2 CUPS RED WINE (OPTIONAL)

FRESH HERB BOUQUET OF 1 BAY LEAF, 2 SPRIGS OF THYME, AND 4 PARSLEY STALKS, TIED WITH KITCHEN TWINE

10 BLACK PEPPERCORNS

3 GARLIC CLOVES

2 TABLESPOONS TOMATO PASTE

Preheat the oven to 450°F. Place the bones in a roasting pan and cook for 45 minutes. Add the onions, carrots, and celery to the roasting pan and cook for 30 minutes more.

Transfer the bones and vegetables to a heavy 8-quart stockpot. Deglaze the roasting pan with some of the water to get all of the browned bits from the bottom of the pan and add this, along with the rest of the water, to the stockpot. Add the optional red wine, herb bouquet, peppercorns, garlic cloves, and tomato paste. Bring to a boil, reduce the heat to low, and carefully skim off any scum that rises to the top. Cover and simmer for 1 to 2 hours. Remove the cover and simmer for 2 to 3 hours more.

Strain the stock and discard the solids. Allow the stock to cool to room temperature, then refrigerate for several hours or overnight. Carefully remove the layer of hardened fat from the surface. (Alternatively, use the quick method of defatting stock, page 3.) Stock will keep for 2 to 3 days refrigerated and for up to 2 months frozen. Defrost overnight in the refrigerator.

Homemade Bouillon Cubes

After the stock has been strained and defatted, it can be returned to the stockpot and simmered over very low heat until it reduces to about 1 to 1½ cups. The resulting liquid, called a *demiglaze*, is very concentrated in flavor. Pour it into a shallow pan, preferably square, and allow it to congeal. Cut into cubes and place them on a parchment-lined baking sheet. Put the baking sheet in the freezer until each cube is solid, then place the cubes in zip-top freezer bags. (This process will keep them from sticking together.) Use these instead of those overly salty store-bought bouillon cubes.

CLASSIC FISH STOCK

Many recipes call for clam juice or clam broth as a substitute for fish stock, but, if at all possible, try to make your own fish stock. The difference in flavor between a fish stock and bottled clam juice is tremendous. A good homemade fish stock is fresh and briny, without the overpowering taste and smell of fish. This stock simmers for only about 30 minutes to ensure a light and delicate taste.

Makes 1½ quarts

3 POUNDS NONOILY (SUCH AS RED SNAPPER, CATFISH, OR TILAPIA) FISH BONES AND/OR CRUSTACEAN SHELLS

1½ QUARTS WATER

1 CUP WHITE WINE

JUICE OF 1 LEMON

4 SHALLOTS, HALVED (UNPEELED)

3 GREEN ONIONS, CHOPPED

1 CARROT, CUT IN HALF

FRESH HERB BOUQUET OF 1 BAY LEAF, 2 SPRIGS OF THYME, AND 4 PARSLEY STALKS, TIED WITH KITCHEN TWINE

10 BLACK PEPPERCORNS

In a heavy 8-quart stockpot, combine all ingredients. Bring to a boil, reduce the heat to low, and carefully skim off any scum that rises to the top. Simmer, uncovered, for 30 minutes.

Strain the stock and discard the solids. Allow the stock to cool to room temperature. Carefully skim any fat from the surface. Stock will keep for 1 to 2 days refrigerated and for up to 1 month frozen. Defrost overnight in the refrigerator.

CLASSIC VEGETABLE STOCK

This stock can be made with what I call "mustgoes." A "mustgo" is not some exotic ingredient, but any vegetable in your refrigerator crisper that is past its prime. This economical, low-fat stock makes a good alternative to water and will enhance any soup, stew, rice dish, sauce, or gravy.

Makes 2 quarts

2 TABLESPOONS OLIVE OIL

3 LEEKS, CLEANED, TRIMMED, AND THINLY SLICED

3 ONIONS, QUARTERED (UNPEELED)

6 GARLIC CLOVES, PEELED

2 YELLOW SQUASH, SLICED

2 ZUCCHINI, SLICED

2 CARROTS, THINLY SLICED

2 RIBS OF CELERY, THINLY SLICED

1 CUP SLICED MUSHROOMS

3½ QUARTS WATER

FRESH HERB BOUQUET OF 1 BAY LEAF, 2 SPRIGS OF THYME,
   AND 4 PARSLEY STALKS, TIED WITH KITCHEN TWINE

10 BLACK PEPPERCORNS

In a heavy 8-quart stockpot over medium-high heat, heat the olive oil and add the leeks, onions, garlic cloves, squash, zucchini, carrots, celery, and mushrooms. Cook, stirring often, until the vegetables are soft but not browned, about 10 to 15 minutes. Add the water, herb bouquet, and peppercorns. Bring to a boil, reduce the heat to low, cover, and simmer for 2 hours. Remove the cover and simmer for 1 hour more.

Strain the stock and discard the solids. Allow the stock to cool to room temperature, then refrigerate for several hours or overnight. Carefully remove any hardened fat from the surface. Stock will keep for 2 to 3 days refrigerated and for up to 2 months frozen. Defrost overnight in the refrigerator.

Ingredients

Because main-course soups should be rich, flavorful creations, you will find that some of these recipes call for a generous number of ingredients. I believe in the concept of "layering" simple flavors and ingredients to create a more complex taste sensation. Many of these ingredients are common ones you should already have in your pantry, such as spices and condiments, and most of them can be easily found at your local farmers market or grocery store. Once you have your ingredients assembled, you will find the soup making uncomplicated and — most important — enjoyable.

Herbs

Whenever possible and for best results, I cook with fresh herbs. Once tough to find outside gourmet stores (or your own garden), fresh herbs are now available at most grocery stores and farmers markets. Use only the leaves of the herb, as the stalks and stems are too strong in flavor and woody in texture. Whenever a recipe calls for fresh parsley, use the Italian flat-leaf variety if possible. It has remarkably more flavor than its curly relative. I find that parsley acts as a flavor enhancer, helping to balance and bring out the taste of other herbs and seasonings. Dried parsley has no resemblance in flavor or texture to its fresh counterpart and, in my opinion, is a waste of money. In cooking school we were taught to chop the herbs until we no longer recognized them. Over the years I have relaxed that standard. Chop as finely or as coarsely as you desire.

If you must use dried herbs in these recipes, use half to one-third the amounts of fresh herbs that the recipe calls for. To help release the essential oils in dried herbs, measure and then briskly rub them between the palms of your hands. If a dried herb no longer has an aroma, chances are it has no flavor either and should be discarded. An absolute no-no in my kitchen is dried rosemary. The brittle twigs never seem to soften during cooking. They remind me of the parched Christmas tree needles I find in my carpet several months after the holidays, with about as much taste.

Onions

Unless a recipe in this book specifically calls for a red onion, use the basic yellow variety. (When they are in season, a mild, sweet-tasting Vidalia, Walla Walla, or Maui onion makes a nice substitute.) You will notice that the recipes that include sliced (not chopped) onion call for the onion to be "halved, peeled, and sliced." I find that the following method of slicing onions both makes the task easier and helps prevent tears: Cut the onion in half lengthwise, placing the cut sides down on the cutting board (away from your nose and eyes). Peel the onion half from the blossom end to the root end, leaving the whole peel intact at the root end. This peel becomes an easy anchor to hold onto when slicing. Then, rocking your knife back and forth, thinly slice the onion until you get to the root end. Your knife should be in contact with the cutting board at all times; viewed from the side, your slicing arm in motion should resemble the turning wheel of a locomotive engine.

If the recipe calls for the onion to be chopped, begin by cutting the onion in half lengthwise and peeling as described above. Slice lengthwise, *making sure you do not cut all the way through the root end.* Then slice crosswise as described above. Save the root end with the peel and use it for making stock. Vegetable trimmings such as root ends and peels impart a wonderful flavor and color to stock.

Beans

Several recipes in this book call for using dried beans. Begin preparing these beans for cooking the night before making the soup. Spread the dried beans on a baking sheet and pick out any debris, little pebbles, or dirt. Rinse the beans very well under cold running water until the water runs clear. Place the beans in a large stainless-steel or glass bowl and cover with one to two inches of water. Allow the beans to soak overnight, changing the water two to three times if possible. Drain and discard the soaking liquid. Refresh the beans under cold running water before using. This presoaking helps to plump the dried beans before cooking and also aids in removing the complex sugars that are difficult to digest.

If time is short, you can use the quick-soak method: After picking through and rinsing the beans, place them in a large stockpot or Dutch oven, then fill with twice as much water as beans. Bring to a boil, reduce heat, cover, and simmer for five minutes. Remove from the heat and let the beans soak for one hour before draining, rinsing, and refreshing.

Storing and Freezing Soup

I have made the majority of these recipes to serve eight as a main-course. If you are cooking for a smaller gathering, make the whole amount and freeze the remainder or enjoy leftovers during the busy week ahead. Quick soup lunches and simmered bowlfuls for supper will help you keep your sanity in this sometimes hectic and hurried world. Most of these soups will keep for two to three days refrigerated and for up to two to three months frozen. Defrost overnight in the refrigerator. The rule of thumb when freezing a soup from this book is this: If the soup contains a stirring of milk, cream, or cheese at the end, prepare the soup up to that point. Ladle out what you plan to use for that particular meal and then use adjusted proportions of the final ingredients to complete the soup. Freeze the remainder without the dairy products, as they tend to get watery or to separate when defrosted. Add these ingredients after defrosting and upon gently reheating. To impart an added boost of flavor, add a sprinkling of freshly chopped herbs when reheating the soup.

POULTRY SOUPS

Dilly Chicken Noodle Soup

Curried Chicken, Wild Rice, and Apple Soup

Old-Fashioned Chicken Soup with Dumplings

Hot and Sour Oriental Chicken Soup

Hectic Holiday Turkey Soup

Chicken Coconut Soup with Galangal

Chicken and Sausage Gumbo

Citrus Chicken and Sun-Dried Tomato Pesto Soup

Chinese-Style Chicken Corn Soup

South of the Border Spicy Turkey Soup

Chicken and Shiitake Mushroom Soup with Wild Rice

Turkey, Mushroom, and Cheddar Soup with
Cheese Doodle Breadsticks

Chicken, Tortilla, and Avocado Soup

DILLY CHICKEN NOODLE SOUP

I love the simple goodness of homemade chicken soup. Fresh dill is a favorite of mine, but if you don't like it, substitute another herb, such as tarragon, basil, chervil, or cilantro. Chopped hard-cooked egg may be sprinkled on the soup if desired.

Serves 6 to 8

1 (4 POUND) CHICKEN, CUT INTO 8 PIECES

ABOUT 12 CUPS WATER

1 ONION, PEELED AND QUARTERED

1 CARROT, SLICED INTO ½-INCH PIECES

1 RIB OF CELERY, SLICED INTO ½-INCH PIECES

1 BAY LEAF, CRUMBLED

1 TEASPOON BLACK PEPPER

1 TEASPOON SALT

FRESH HERB BOUQUET OF 1 SPRIG EACH OF PARSLEY, SAGE, ROSEMARY, AND THYME, TIED WITH KITCHEN TWINE

1 (16 OUNCE) PACKAGE EGG NOODLES

2 TO 3 TABLESPOONS CHOPPED FRESH DILL

Place the chicken in a heavy 8-quart stockpot with enough water to cover the pieces by 1 inch. Add the onion, carrot, celery, bay leaf, pepper, salt, and fresh herb bouquet. Bring to a boil, reduce the heat, and gently simmer for 1 hour. Skim away any scum that rises to the top.

Remove the chicken from the stockpot. When cool enough to handle, remove the meat from the bone. Dice the meat into small pieces and set aside.

Strain the broth and discard the vegetables and herbs. If desired, briefly chill the broth and skim away any fat that rises to the top.

Return the broth to the stockpot and bring to a boil. Boil until the broth reduces to about 8 cups. Add the egg noodles and cook for 8 to 10 minutes, or until tender. Stir in the diced chicken and chopped dill. Simmer until the chicken is reheated, about 2 minutes. Taste and adjust seasonings with additional salt and pepper if necessary. Serve at once.

CURRIED CHICKEN, WILD RICE & APPLE SOUP

The flavors in this soup are similar to those found in Country Captain, a classic Southern dish of chicken served over rice. (Country Captain was said to be FDR's favorite when he was recuperating in Warm Springs, Georgia.) Sautéing the curry powder with the vegetables helps to lessen the sometimes overpowering taste of this spice blend.

Serves 8

4 CUPS COOKED, COARSELY CHOPPED CHICKEN

½ CUP MANGO CHUTNEY, SUCH AS MAJOR GREY'S

½ CUP SLIVERED ALMONDS, LIGHTLY TOASTED*

3 TABLESPOONS BUTTER

3 TABLESPOONS OLIVE OIL

2 ONIONS, FINELY CHOPPED

2 GARLIC CLOVES, FINELY CHOPPED

3 RIBS OF CELERY, FINELY CHOPPED

2 TABLESPOONS SWEET OR MILD CURRY POWDER,
  PREFERABLY MADRAS

¼ TEASPOON CAYENNE PEPPER

1 CUP GOLDEN RAISINS

1 (28 OUNCE) CAN CHOPPED TOMATOES WITH THEIR JUICE

8 CUPS CHICKEN STOCK, PREFERABLY HOMEMADE

2 CUPS COOKED WILD RICE

2 GOLDEN DELICIOUS APPLES, CORED AND CUT INTO
  SMALL CHUNKS

¼ CUP CHOPPED FRESH PARSLEY

2 TABLESPOONS LEMON JUICE

SALT AND FRESHLY GROUND BLACK PEPPER

In a large bowl, combine the cooked, chopped chicken, mango chutney, and slivered almonds. Mix well and set aside.

In a 4½-quart Dutch oven over medium-high heat, melt the butter with the olive oil until hot. Add the onions, garlic, and celery. Cook, stirring often, until the onions begin to wilt, about 5 minutes. Stir in the curry powder and cayenne pepper. Cook for 2 minutes. Add the raisins and the tomatoes with their juice. Cook for 10 minutes, stirring often to prevent sticking.

Add the chicken stock, wild rice, apples, parsley, and lemon juice. Stir in the cooked chicken and chutney-almond mixture. Bring to a boil, reduce the heat, and simmer for 3 to 5 minutes, or until the apples are crisp-tender. Season to taste with salt and pepper.

Serve hot, with assorted crackers or breadsticks.

*To toast nuts, preheat the oven to 350°F. Spread the nuts on a baking sheet, place in the oven, and toast, stirring occasionally, for 6 to 8 minutes, or until golden brown.

OLD-FASHIONED CHICKEN SOUP WITH DUMPLINGS

This humble comfort food is now appearing on some of the most chic menus in the country.
Once you give it a try, you'll understand why.

Serves 8 to 10

Meat and Broth

1 (4 POUND) CHICKEN, CUT INTO 8 PIECES

ABOUT 3 QUARTS WATER

3 ONIONS, PEELED AND QUARTERED

3 CARROTS, SLICED INTO ½-INCH PIECES

3 RIBS OF CELERY, SLICED INTO ½-INCH PIECES

1 BAY LEAF, CRUMBLED

½ TEASPOON BLACK PEPPER

1 TEASPOON SALT

FRESH HERB BOUQUET MADE WITH 1 SPRIG EACH OF
PARSLEY, SAGE, ROSEMARY, AND THYME, TIED WITH
KITCHEN TWINE

Dumplings

3 CUPS ALL-PURPOSE SOFT WINTER WHEAT (SOUTHERN)
FLOUR, SUCH AS WHITE LILY

½ TEASPOON BAKING SODA

½ TEASPOON SALT

1 TEASPOON POULTRY SEASONING

6 TABLESPOONS CHILLED SHORTENING

¼ CUP OF THE CHICKEN BROTH

⅔ CUP BUTTERMILK

SALT AND FRESHLY GROUND BLACK PEPPER

Place the chicken in a heavy 5½-quart Dutch oven with enough water to cover by 1 inch. Add the onions, carrots, celery, bay leaf, pepper, salt, and fresh herb bouquet. Bring to a boil, reduce the heat, and simmer for 1 hour. Skim away any scum that rises to the top.

Remove the chicken from the pot. When cool enough to handle, remove the meat from the bone and set aside. Strain the broth and add the vegetables to the meat. Discard the herb bouquet. Briefly chill the broth and skim away any fat that rises to the top.

To make the dumplings, sift together the flour, baking soda, salt, and poultry seasoning in a large bowl. With a pastry blender, two knives, or a fork, cut the shortening into the flour until it resembles a coarse meal. Make a well in the center of the flour and add ¼ cup of the chicken broth and the buttermilk. Stir to make a stiff dough. Turn the dough onto a lightly floured counter and knead gently 8 to 10 times. Pat the dough into a round, wrap in plastic wrap, and refrigerate for 1 hour.

Bring the remaining broth to a slow simmer. Roll the chilled dough on a lightly floured counter until it is about ¼-inch thick. Add additional flour to the counter if the dough begins to stick. Cut the dough into 4 x 1-inch strips. Add the strips, one at a time, to the simmering broth. When all the dough has been added to the broth, gently stir and cook for 10 to 12 minutes, or until the dumplings are firm yet tender (al dente). Add the reserved chicken and vegetables to the pot. Season with additional salt and freshly ground pepper if needed. Serve at once.

HOT & SOUR ORIENTAL CHICKEN SOUP

Chicken soup is said to be a cure-all. If that's true, then this version is a secret weapon. I'm not making any medical claims, but if you are feeling a bit sluggish and your head is all stuffed up, the soothing warmth from the chicken broth and the chile garlic paste, along with the bright, fresh taste of the ginger, will provide some much-needed relief and comfort, even if it is all in your head.

Serves 6 to 8

10 CUPS CHICKEN STOCK, PREFERABLY HOMEMADE

1 (2 INCH) PIECE OF GINGER, PEELED AND CUT INTO
JULIENNE STRIPS

2 BUNCHES GREEN ONIONS, SLICED ON THE DIAGONAL
INTO 1-INCH PIECES

2 RIBS OF CELERY, THINLY SLICED

3 CARROTS, THINLY SLICED

1 CUP SNOW PEAS, TIPPED AND TAILED

1 (6 OUNCE) CAN SLICED WATER CHESTNUTS, DRAINED

2 CUPS COOKED, SHREDDED CHICKEN

3 TABLESPOONS SOY SAUCE

1 TABLESPOON HOISIN SAUCE

1 TABLESPOON CHILE GARLIC PASTE

3 TABLESPOONS RICE WINE VINEGAR

1 TEASPOON BROWN SUGAR

FRESHLY GROUND BLACK PEPPER

1 EGG, BEATEN

Place the chicken stock in a 4½-quart Dutch oven and bring to a boil. Add the ginger, green onions, celery, and carrots. Cook over medium heat for about 10 minutes. Add the snow peas and the water chestnuts and continue cooking for 2 minutes. Stir in the chicken, soy sauce, Hoisin sauce, chile garlic paste, rice wine vinegar, brown sugar, and black pepper. Slowly whisk in the beaten egg. Continue whisking until the egg is cooked and forms long threads. Serve at once.

This soup freezes fine for leftovers but is best when made the day it is served.

HECTIC HOLIDAY TURKEY SOUP

After holiday meals, I'm always left with a couple of potatoes, a bit of stuffing, or a half-filled bowl of cranberry sauce. This recipe takes some of those leftovers and combines them into a very satisfying soup that's a perfect antidote to frenzied holiday shopping. The longer the turkey bones cook, the better tasting the broth will be.

Serves 8

1 TURKEY CARCASS

ABOUT 12 TO 15 CUPS WATER

1 ONION, PEELED AND QUARTERED

1 CARROT, SLICED INTO ½-INCH PIECES

1 RIB OF CELERY, SLICED INTO ½-INCH PIECES

1 BAY LEAF, CRUMBLED

1 TEASPOON BLACK PEPPER

1 TEASPOON SALT

FRESH HERB BOUQUET OF 1 SPRIG EACH OF PARSLEY, SAGE, ROSEMARY, AND THYME, TIED WITH KITCHEN TWINE

2 ONIONS, HALVED, PEELED, AND THINLY SLICED

1 SWEET POTATO, PEELED AND CUT INTO ½-INCH DICE

1 BAKING POTATO, PEELED AND CUT INTO ½-INCH DICE

1 (16 OUNCE) PACKAGE FROZEN BUTTER PEAS OR LIMA BEANS

1 TABLESPOON CHOPPED FRESH SAGE

2 TEASPOONS POULTRY SEASONING

½ CUP HERBED OR CORN BREAD STUFFING MIX, SUCH AS PEPPERIDGE FARM

½ CUP WHOLE-BERRY CRANBERRY SAUCE

Place the turkey carcass in a heavy 5½-quart Dutch oven with enough water to cover the bones by 1 inch. Add the quartered onion, carrot, celery, bay leaf, pepper, salt, and fresh herb bouquet. Bring to a boil, reduce the heat, and gently simmer for 2 hours. Skim away any scum that rises to the top.

Remove the carcass from the stockpot. When cool enough to handle, remove any meat from the bone. Dice the meat into small pieces and set aside.

Strain the broth and discard the vegetables and herbs. If desired, briefly chill the broth and skim away any fat that rises to the top.

Return the broth to the Dutch oven and bring to a boil. Boil until the broth reduces to about 8 cups. Add the sliced onions, sweet potato, baking potato, butter peas or lima beans, sage, and poultry seasoning. Cover and simmer for 30 minutes, or until potatoes are tender.

Add the reserved turkey meat and stuffing mix. Cook for 10 minutes, or until stuffing mix has absorbed some of the stock and the soup is thick. Adjust seasonings with additional salt and pepper if necessary. Serve at once, with a spoonful of the cranberry sauce garnishing each soup bowl.

CHICKEN COCONUT SOUP WITH GALANGAL

This soup is alive with taste sensations, combining the sweetness of coconut milk, the citrus of lemon grass and lime leaves, the saltiness of fish sauce, and the fire of Thai chiles. It is the perfect soup to wake up your palate from the winter doldrums. Galangal is a rhizome related to ginger. It has a strong, lemony, slightly astringent taste. You can substitute ginger if galangal isn't available, but you should be able to find all these ingredients at any large farmers market or Asian grocery store.

Serves 8

4 STALKS LEMON GRASS, CUT INTO 2-INCH PIECES AND CRUSHED SLIGHTLY

14 QUARTER-SIZED SLICES OF GALANGAL

10 KAFFIR LIME LEAVES

½ TEASPOON CORIANDER SEED

½ TEASPOON BLACK PEPPERCORNS

6 CUPS COCONUT MILK

3 CUPS CHICKEN STOCK, PREFERABLY HOMEMADE

3 BONELESS, SKINLESS CHICKEN BREASTS, CUT INTO BITE-SIZED PIECES

2 CUPS STRAW OR ENOKI MUSHROOMS, RINSED AND DRAINED

3 TABLESPOONS FISH SAUCE

3 TABLESPOONS FRESHLY SQUEEZED LIME JUICE

4 THAI BIRD CHILES OR SERRANO CHILES, VERY THINLY SLICED

Tie the lemon grass, galangal, Kaffir lime leaves, coriander seed, and black peppercorns together in a large piece of cheesecloth.

In a 4½-quart Dutch oven over medium heat, combine the coconut milk and chicken stock. Bring to a low simmer and add the chicken pieces and the cheesecloth containing the flavorings. Gently cook for 15 to 18 minutes, or until the chicken is opaque and cooked through.

Discard the cheesecloth and its contents. Remove the pot from the heat and stir in the mushrooms, fish sauce, and lime juice. Taste and adjust seasonings, adding additional fish sauce and lime juice if you like. Stir in the sliced chiles.

Ladle into bowls and serve at once.

CHICKEN & SAUSAGE GUMBO

This gumbo recipe utilizes what Paul Prudhomme calls the trinity of Cajun cooking: onions, garlic, and green peppers. This is a wonderful dish to make ahead. If you like, drizzle each bowlful with a little apple cider vinegar before serving. Ice-cold beer is a refreshing accompaniment to this spicy dish.

Serves 8 to 10

⅓ cup vegetable oil

⅓ cup flour

3 onions, chopped

2 green peppers, seeded and chopped

6 garlic cloves, chopped

1 pound okra, sliced, or 1 (16 ounce) frozen package, defrosted

10 cups chicken stock, preferably homemade

6 boneless, skinless chicken breasts, cut into 1-inch cubes

2 pounds smoked polish or kielbasa sausage, sliced

1 cup long-grain rice

1 (28 ounce) can chopped tomatoes with their juice

2 tablespoons Worcestershire sauce

1 teaspoon Tabasco

Salt and freshly ground black pepper

1 bay leaf, crumbled

1 tablespoon thyme leaves

½ cup chopped fresh parsley

Additional Tabasco

In a heavy 8-quart stockpot, combine the oil and the flour and cook over medium heat, stirring constantly, until the roux is a dark caramel color, about 20 minutes. Be very careful not to burn the roux or a scorched taste will pervade the gumbo.

Stir in the onions, green peppers, and garlic and cook for an additional 20 minutes, stirring occasionally. Stir in the okra and cook for 3 minutes. (At this stage the mixture can be cooled, packed in a zip-top freezer bag, and refrigerated or frozen for later use.)

Add the chicken stock, chicken breasts, kielbasa, rice, tomatoes, Worcestershire sauce, Tabasco, salt and pepper to taste, bay leaf, and thyme leaves. Bring the mixture to a boil, cover, and reduce the heat to a simmer. Cook for 30 minutes, stirring occasionally.

Just before serving, add the parsley. Pass the Tabasco separately.

CITRUS CHICKEN & SUN-DRIED TOMATO PESTO SOUP

The beauty of this soup is that it can be made entirely ahead of time and assembled two minutes before serving. I love to make this in the waning days of winter, when I am longing for lighter-tasting fare. Traditionally, pesto is an uncooked sauce made with fresh basil, garlic, pine nuts, Parmesan cheese, and olive oil. I call the sauce for this soup a "pesto" because the basic preparation technique remains the same.

Serves 8

4 BONELESS, SKINLESS CHICKEN BREASTS

JUICE AND GRATED ZEST OF 1 ORANGE

JUICE AND GRATED ZEST OF 1 LEMON

JUICE AND GRATED ZEST OF 1 LIME

1 CUP SUN-DRIED TOMATOES, RECONSTITUTED IN 2 CUPS OF BOILING WATER AND DRAINED WELL

6 GARLIC CLOVES, PEELED

1 CUP SEASONED BREAD CRUMBS

1 CUP GRATED ROMANO CHEESE

1 CUP WALNUTS, LIGHTLY TOASTED (SEE PAGE 13)

1 TABLESPOON CHOPPED FRESH ROSEMARY

2 TABLESPOONS CHOPPED FRESH BASIL

¼ CUP CHOPPED FRESH PARSLEY

SALT AND FRESHLY GROUND BLACK PEPPER

⅔ CUP EXTRA-VIRGIN OLIVE OIL

8 CUPS CHICKEN STOCK, PREFERABLY HOMEMADE

2 CUPS BEAN SPROUTS

Place the boneless, skinless chicken breasts in a large bowl. Add the citrus juices and zest and let marinate at room temperature for 1 hour. Preheat the broiler. Place the chicken on a broiler rack and cook for 15 to 18 minutes, turning the chicken once during the process. Transfer the chicken to a cutting board and allow to sit for 10 minutes. Thinly slice and set aside.

Meanwhile, in a food processor, combine the reconstituted tomatoes, garlic, bread crumbs, Romano cheese, walnuts, rosemary, basil, parsley, and salt and pepper to taste. Process until finely chopped. Add the olive oil in a thin steady stream and process until smooth. Set aside.

In a 4½-quart Dutch oven, bring the chicken stock to a boil. Divide the chicken strips, bean sprouts, and 1 to 2 tablespoons of the pesto sauce among 8 serving bowls. Add 1 cup of the boiling stock to each bowl and stir. Serve at once.

CHINESE-STYLE CHICKEN CORN SOUP

What a perfect way to ring in the Chinese New Year. This recipe is an adaptation of a soup from my favorite wok wizard, Shirley Fong-Torres, and can easily be prepared in a large, well-seasoned wok. Don't use chopsticks, though!

Serves 8

4 BONELESS, SKINLESS CHICKEN BREASTS, THINLY SLICED

1 EGG WHITE, BEATEN UNTIL FROTHY

1 TABLESPOON RICE WINE (NOT VINEGAR) OR SHERRY

3 TABLESPOONS SOY SAUCE

2 TABLESPOONS HOISIN SAUCE

1 TABLESPOON CHOPPED FRESH GINGER

½ TEASPOON FIVE-SPICE POWDER

2 TEASPOONS CORNSTARCH

2 TABLESPOONS DARK ASIAN SESAME OIL

FRESHLY GROUND BLACK PEPPER

8 CUPS CHICKEN STOCK, PREFERABLY HOMEMADE

2 (15½ OUNCE) CANS CREAM-STYLE CORN

1 (6½ OUNCE) CAN SLICED WATER CHESTNUTS, DRAINED

1 RED PEPPER, SEEDED AND CHOPPED

½ CUP CHOPPED SMITHFIELD OR COUNTRY HAM (OPTIONAL)

2 EGGS, LIGHTLY BEATEN

1 TABLESPOON CORNSTARCH MIXED WITH 2 TABLESPOONS
    WATER

6 GREEN ONIONS, CHOPPED

DARK ASIAN SESAME OIL FOR DRIZZLING (OPTIONAL)

Place the chicken in a medium glass bowl and toss with the egg white. Add the rice wine or sherry, soy sauce, Hoisin sauce, ginger, five-spice powder, cornstarch, sesame oil, and black pepper to taste. Cover, refrigerate, and let marinate for 1 hour.

In a large 5½-quart Dutch oven, bring the chicken stock to a boil. Immediately add the chicken and stir to prevent any pieces from sticking together. Cook over medium-high heat for 5 minutes. Stir in the corn, water chestnuts, and red pepper. Continue cooking for 5 minutes, or until the chicken turns white and is cooked through. Add the optional country ham and cook for 2 minutes more.

Reduce the heat to low and gently swirl the beaten eggs in a slow, steady stream into the soup. Add the cornstarch-water mixture to thicken. When the egg is cooked (it will form threads), the soup is ready. Top with green onions and drizzle with dark Asian sesame oil if desired. Serve at once.

SOUTH OF THE BORDER SPICY TURKEY SOUP

I keep most of the ingredients for this soup on hand, either on the pantry shelf or in the refrigerator. With the demands on my time, a well-stocked pantry, plus a soup that can be ready in less than an hour, makes living in the real world a little easier. For a smokier flavor, substitute chopped chipotle peppers for the jalapeños.

Serves 8

2 teaspoons peanut oil

2 pounds ground turkey

1 onion, chopped

4 garlic cloves, chopped

¼ cup chopped fresh cilantro, divided

2 to 3 tablespoons chili powder

1 tablespoon ground cumin

½ teaspoon cayenne pepper

1 (28 ounce) can chopped tomatoes with their juice

1 (15½ ounce) can Great Northern or white beans, rinsed and drained

1 (15½) can black beans, rinsed and drained

1 (15½ ounce) can creamed corn

2 to 3 jalapeño peppers, fresh or canned, seeded and chopped

8 cups chicken stock, preferably homemade

Salt and freshly ground black pepper

6 green onions, chopped

Sour cream and shredded sharp cheddar cheese

In a 4½-quart Dutch oven, heat the oil over medium-high heat and add the ground turkey, onion, garlic, and 2 tablespoons of the chopped cilantro. Crumble the turkey with a fork and cook until it is no longer pink, about 8 minutes. Drain off the excess fat.

Stir in the chili powder, cumin, and cayenne pepper. Add the chopped tomatoes and their juice, Great Northern or white beans, black beans, creamed corn, jalapeño peppers, chicken stock, and salt and pepper to taste. Simmer, uncovered, for 30 to 40 minutes.

Just before serving, stir in the green onions and the remaining 2 tablespoons of chopped cilantro. Serve immediately, with dollops of sour cream and shredded cheddar cheese on top.

CHICKEN & SHIITAKE MUSHROOM SOUP WITH WILD RICE

Gently poaching the chicken breasts for this soup assures you a fresh-tasting broth and moist, juicy chunks of chicken. An interesting note: Wild rice, with its crunchy texture and appealing, nut-like taste, is not really a rice at all but a wild marsh grass native to North America. Follow the directions on the package of wild rice carefully, as overcooking tends to produce a gummy mess.

Serves 8

4 BONELESS, SKINLESS CHICKEN BREASTS

ABOUT 10 CUPS WATER

1 YELLOW ONION, QUARTERED

1 CARROT, CUT IN HALF

1 RIB OF CELERY, CUT IN HALF

1 BAY LEAF

10 BLACK PEPPERCORNS

SALT AND FRESHLY GROUND BLACK PEPPER

1 TABLESPOON OLIVE OIL

1 RED ONION, THINLY SLICED

2 RIBS OF CELERY, THINLY SLICED

3 CARROTS, SHREDDED

4 GARLIC CLOVES, CHOPPED

2 CUPS THINLY SLICED SHIITAKE MUSHROOMS

¼ CUP FLOUR

1 CUP HALF AND HALF

1 CUP SOUR CREAM

2 CUPS COOKED WILD RICE

2 TABLESPOONS FRESH THYME LEAVES

In a 4½-quart Dutch oven, combine the chicken, water, yellow onion, halved carrot, halved celery rib, bay leaf, peppercorns, and salt and pepper to taste. Bring to a boil, reduce the heat to low, and carefully skim off any scum that rises to the top. Cover and simmer the chicken for 25 minutes. Remove the chicken from the broth and set aside to cool. Strain the remaining broth, discarding the solids, and place in the refrigerator to chill. When the chicken is cool enough to handle, dice into chunks or bite-sized pieces. Cover and refrigerate until needed.

Meanwhile, in the same Dutch oven, heat the olive oil over medium-high heat until sizzling. Add the red onion, sliced celery, shredded carrots, and garlic and cook for about 5 minutes. Lower the heat to medium, add the mushrooms, and cook for 5 minutes more. Add the flour and salt and pepper to taste and stir to combine. Cook for 2 minutes.

Stir in the chilled chicken stock (after removing the fat that has accumulated at the top) and the half and half. Whisk in the sour cream, stirring until the soup is thickened and heated through. Add the cooked wild rice, shredded chicken, and thyme leaves, stirring until thick and bubbly. Serve at once.

TURKEY, MUSHROOM & CHEDDAR SOUP

Leftovers again? Those dreaded words can haunt all of us. Score points for yourself with this easy and inventive recipe that relies on pantry staples and leftover turkey to infuse new life into a cheesy soup base. Enjoy this with crispy Cheese Doodle Breadsticks.

Serves 8

2 TABLESPOONS OLIVE OIL

2 ONIONS, CHOPPED

3 CARROTS, FINELY DICED

2 RIBS OF CELERY, THINLY SLICED

2 CUPS SLICED BUTTON MUSHROOMS

1 (10 OUNCE) PACKAGE FROZEN TINY ENGLISH PEAS, DEFROSTED

2 GARLIC CLOVES, CHOPPED

6 CUPS CHICKEN STOCK, PREFERABLY HOMEMADE

1 TABLESPOON WORCESTERSHIRE SAUCE

2 TEASPOONS CHOPPED FRESH ROSEMARY

1 TABLESPOON CHOPPED FRESH SAGE

3 TEASPOONS POULTRY SEASONING

SALT AND FRESHLY GROUND BLACK PEPPER

3 CUPS COOKED, SHREDDED TURKEY OR CHICKEN

6 TABLESPOONS BUTTER

⅓ CUP FLOUR

½ TEASPOON SALT

¼ TEASPOON BLACK PEPPER

3 CUPS MILK

2 CUPS GRATED CHEDDAR CHEESE

In a 5½-quart Dutch oven over medium-high heat, heat the oil until sizzling. Add the onions, carrots, celery, mushrooms, peas, and garlic. Cook over medium heat until the onions begin to wilt and the carrots begin to soften, about 10 minutes. Stir in the chicken stock, Worcestershire sauce, rosemary, sage, poultry seasoning, salt and pepper to taste, and shredded turkey or chicken. Bring to a boil, reduce the heat, and simmer for 15 minutes.

In a medium saucepan, melt the butter and add the flour, salt, and pepper. Cook over low heat, stirring all the time, until mixture is smooth and bubbly. Add the milk, bring to a boil, and cook for 1 minute. Remove from the heat and add the cheese, stirring until it is melted and smooth.

Pour the cheese sauce into the soup and gently heat for 2 to 3 minutes, or until thickened. Taste and add salt and pepper if necessary. Serve at once.

CHEESE DOODLE BREADSTICKS

These crunchy breadsticks freeze very nicely for up to three months. They have all the taste of a traditional Southern cheese straw minus the fuss.

Makes about 2 dozen

½ PACKAGE (1 SHEET) FROZEN PUFF PASTRY, THAWED

1 EGG WHITE, BEATEN LIGHTLY

½ CUP GRATED CHEDDAR CHEESE

½ CUP GRATED PARMESAN CHEESE

¼ TEASPOON CAYENNE PEPPER

Preheat the oven to 425°F. Unfold the pastry sheet and brush it all over with the egg white. Sprinkle on the grated cheeses and cayenne pepper. Fold the sheet in half crosswise and press or roll with a rolling pin until it is flat.

Turn the pastry so that it is facing you lengthwise. Cut into thin strips, about ½ inch wide, and twist each strip in opposite directions several times. Place on a baking sheet and bake for about 10 to 12 minutes. With a spatula, remove the twists to a wire rack to cool. They are ready to eat as soon as they are cool enough to handle.

CHICKEN, TORTILLA & AVOCADO SOUP

Pico de gallo, a chunky salsa of tomatoes, peppers, onions, lime juice, and cilantro, literally translated means "rooster's beak." It supposedly got its name because it was originally eaten with the thumb and pointer finger in a motion that resembled a pecking rooster. The pico de gallo adds a surprisingly fresh and wholesome taste to this hearty soup. The recipe has been loosely adapted from a recipe by Linda Hopkins of Les Gourmettes Cooking School in Phoenix, Arizona.

Serves 8

2 TABLESPOONS CORN OIL

6 CORN TORTILLAS, CUT INTO THIN STRIPS

1 RED ONION, FINELY CHOPPED

4 GARLIC CLOVES, CHOPPED

2 JALAPEÑO PEPPERS, SEEDED AND CHOPPED

1 (28 OUNCE) CAN CHOPPED TOMATOES WITH THEIR JUICE

2 TABLESPOONS CHILI POWDER

1 TABLESPOON GROUND CUMIN

¼ TEASPOON CAYENNE PEPPER

6 CUPS CHICKEN STOCK, PREFERABLY HOMEMADE

1 (8 OUNCE) CAN RED ENCHILADA SAUCE

3 CUPS COOKED, SHREDDED CHICKEN

½ CUP CHOPPED FRESH CILANTRO

1 RIPE AVOCADO, PEELED, PITTED, AND CUT INTO CHUNKS

1 CUP SHREDDED MONTEREY JACK CHEESE

Pico de Gallo

2 RIPE TOMATOES, SEEDED AND FINELY CHOPPED

1 ONION, FINELY CHOPPED

3 GREEN ONIONS, FINELY CHOPPED

2 TABLESPOONS PEANUT OIL

1 JALAPEÑO PEPPER, SEEDED AND FINELY CHOPPED

3 TABLESPOONS FINELY CHOPPED FRESH CILANTRO

3 TABLESPOONS LIME JUICE

SALT AND FRESHLY GROUND BLACK PEPPER

In a 4½-quart Dutch oven, heat the corn oil over medium-high heat until sizzling. Add the tortillas, reduce the heat to medium, and cook until they are golden brown. Add the onion, garlic, and jalapeños. Cook until the onion is soft, about 3 to 4 minutes. Stir in the chopped tomatoes, chili powder, cumin, and cayenne pepper. Cook for 10 minutes.

Stir in the chicken stock and enchilada sauce. Simmer, uncovered, for 10 minutes. Stir in the chicken, cilantro, and avocado. Cook for 2 minutes, or until just heated.

To serve, ladle into individual bowls and top with pico de gallo and shredded Monterey Jack cheese. Serve with tortilla chips on the side.

Pico de Gallo

In a medium bowl, mix together all the ingredients. Let sit at room temperature for 1 hour before using to allow the flavors to mellow. Refrigerate unused portion for up to 5 days.

Note: It is very important to do all of your chopping for the pico de gallo by hand. Chopping the vegetables in the food processor will make the salsa too watery.

MEAT SOUPS

Osso Buco Soup Milanese

Lamb, Smoked Sausage, and White Bean Soup

German Potato Soup

Marge's Artichoke and Sausage Soup

New England Corned Beef and Cabbage Soup

Moroccan Lamb Soup with Couscous

Braised Beefy Vegetable Soup

Fiery Thai Grilled Beef Soup

Hearty Reuben Soup

Greek Meatball Soup with Feta and Cucumbers

Creamy Beef Stroganoff Noodle Soup

Florentine Sausage and Pepperoni Soup

Cuban Pork and Mustard Green Soup

Southwestern Pinto Bean Soup

Irish Beef, Cabbage, and Barley Soup

Greek Moussaka Soup

Marinated Steak and Potato Soup

OSSO BUCO SOUP MILANESE

This soup is based on the classic veal shank dish from Milan. Arborio rice, a short-grain Italian rice used for making risotto, is used to thicken the soup. The meat on the veal shanks can be removed prior to serving, but for presentation sake I like to leave it intact. In that case, I set the table with a knife and fork as well as a spoon, but the meat is so tender it literally falls off the bone.

Serves 8

8 MEATY VEAL SHANKS, ABOUT ¾ POUND EACH

SALT AND FRESHLY GROUND BLACK PEPPER

¼ CUP FLOUR

¼ CUP OLIVE OIL

2 ONIONS, CHOPPED

3 CARROTS, COARSELY CHOPPED

2 RIBS OF CELERY, THINLY SLICED

3 GARLIC CLOVES, CHOPPED

1 CUP RED WINE

1 (28 OUNCE) CAN CHOPPED TOMATOES WITH THEIR JUICE

½ CUP ARBORIO RICE

8 CUPS BEEF STOCK, PREFERABLY HOMEMADE

2 BAY LEAVES, CRUMBLED

2 TABLESPOONS CHOPPED FRESH BASIL

3 TABLESPOONS TOMATO PASTE

GRATED ZEST OF 3 ORANGES

4 GARLIC CLOVES, CHOPPED

½ CUP FRESHLY GRATED PARMESAN CHEESE

½ CUP CHOPPED FRESH PARSLEY

Preheat the oven to 350°F. Season the veal shanks with salt and pepper and dredge on both sides in the flour. In a 5½-quart Dutch oven, heat the oil over medium-high heat until sizzling. Add the veal shanks and brown on both sides, about 3 minutes per side. Remove to a plate.

In the same Dutch oven, add the onions, carrots, celery, and 3 cloves of chopped garlic. Cook over medium heat for about 10 minutes to soften the vegetables. Stir in the red wine, chopped tomatoes, Arborio rice, beef stock, bay leaves, basil, and tomato paste. Return the shanks to the pot. Bring to a boil, cover the pot, and place in the oven to continue cooking. Cook for 1½ to 2 hours, or until the shanks are fork-tender.

Meanwhile, in a small bowl, mix together the orange zest, 4 cloves of chopped garlic, Parmesan cheese, and parsley. Set aside.

Place 1 shank into each of 8 shallow serving bowls. Adjust seasonings with salt and pepper and spoon the soup base over and around the shanks. Sprinkle with the parsley mixture. Serve at once.

LAMB, SMOKED SAUSAGE & WHITE BEAN SOUP

This soup has all the traditional flavors of a cassoulet but without the day-long fuss required for the classic French dish. (Some recipes take up to three days.) The quick wilting of the spinach in the final step adds beautiful streaks of green color to the finished soup.

Serves 8 to 10

2 TABLESPOONS OLIVE OIL

1 TEASPOON ALLSPICE

1 POUND BONELESS LAMB SHOULDER, CUT INTO 1-INCH
    CUBES AND FAT REMOVED

2 POUNDS SMOKED POLISH OR KIELBASA SAUSAGE, CUT
    INTO 1-INCH PIECES

3 ONIONS, CHOPPED

6 GARLIC CLOVES, CHOPPED

3 CARROTS, THINLY SLICED

1 (28 OUNCE) CAN PLUM TOMATOES WITH THEIR JUICE

2 CUPS RED WINE

8 CUPS BEEF STOCK, PREFERABLY HOMEMADE

2 TEASPOONS POULTRY SEASONING

¼ TEASPOON CAYENNE PEPPER

SALT AND FRESHLY GROUND BLACK PEPPER

2 (15½ OUNCE) CANS GREAT NORTHERN OR WHITE BEANS,
    RINSED AND DRAINED

2 BAY LEAVES, CRUMBLED

½ CUP CHOPPED FRESH PARSLEY

2 TABLESPOONS CHOPPED FRESH BASIL

1 (10 OUNCE) PACKAGE WASHED SPINACH LEAVES, STEMS
    REMOVED

In a 5½-quart Dutch oven over medium-high heat, heat the olive oil and stir in the allspice. Add the lamb pieces and brown on all sides. Remove lamb from the pot and place in a large bowl. Add the smoked sausage to the pot and cook, stirring occasionally, until browned around the edges, about 5 to 7 minutes. Remove from the pot and place in the bowl with the lamb.

Remove all but about 2 tablespoons of the reserved drippings from the pot and discard. In the reserved drippings, cook the onions, garlic, and carrots over medium heat until soft, about 10 minutes. Add the tomatoes with their juice, coarsely breaking them up with the back of a spoon. Add the red wine and beef stock. Stir in the browned meats and any meat juices that have accumulated in the bowl. Bring to a boil, reduce the heat to a simmer, cover, and cook for about 20 minutes.

Remove the cover and add the poultry seasoning, cayenne pepper, salt and pepper to taste, white beans, bay leaves, parsley, and basil. Simmer, uncovered, for 20 minutes. (The soup can be made ahead to this point and refrigerated for several days or frozen for up to 3 months.)

Just before serving, stir in washed spinach and adjust the seasonings with additional salt and pepper. The spinach will wilt and cook down in about 3 minutes. Serve at once.

GERMAN POTATO SOUP

I like to serve this soup with dark pumpernickel bread and additional coarse-grained mustard at the table. A stout German beer is strong enough, flavor-wise, to hold its own when served with this robust soup.

Serves 8

3 POUNDS MEDIUM-SIZED NEW POTATOES, SCRUBBED AND
   THICKLY SLICED

8 STRIPS OF BACON, COARSELY CHOPPED

3 ONIONS, CHOPPED

4 GARLIC CLOVES, CHOPPED

3 RIBS OF CELERY, THINLY SLICED

1 CUP THINLY SLICED RADISHES

⅓ CUP APPLE CIDER VINEGAR

⅓ CUP COARSE-GRAINED DIJON MUSTARD

2 TEASPOONS CARAWAY SEED, SLIGHTLY CRUSHED

2 TABLESPOONS CHOPPED FRESH MARJORAM

½ TEASPOON ALLSPICE

½ TEASPOON GROUND GINGER

2 TABLESPOONS BROWN SUGAR

¼ TEASPOON CAYENNE PEPPER

SALT AND FRESHLY GROUND BLACK PEPPER

8 CUPS BEEF STOCK, PREFERABLY HOMEMADE

3 TABLESPOONS CHOPPED FRESH CHIVES

Beer-Braised Bratwurst

2 TABLESPOONS VEGETABLE OIL

1 ONION, HALVED, PEELED, AND THINLY SLICED

1 (15½ OUNCE) CAN SAUERKRAUT, RINSED AND DRAINED

4 LARGE, FRESH BRATWURST SAUSAGES, PRICKED
   ALL OVER WITH A FORK

1 (12 OUNCE) BOTTLE DARK BEER

In a 4½-quart Dutch oven, cover the potatoes with enough lightly salted water to submerge them by 3 inches. Bring the water to a boil and cook the potatoes for 15 minutes, or until just tender. Drain and place in a glass bowl. Set aside.

In the same Dutch oven, cook the bacon over medium heat until crisp and browned, remove to a paper towel, and drain. Add the onions, garlic, celery, and radishes to the hot drippings. Cook for 5 minutes, or until the onions are soft. Add the apple cider vinegar, mustard, caraway seed, marjoram, allspice, ginger, brown sugar, cayenne pepper, and salt and pepper to taste. Stir in the beef stock and simmer for 20 minutes.

Meanwhile, make the bratwurst. Heat the vegetable oil in a 12-inch skillet over medium-high heat. Add the onion and sauerkraut and cook until the onion is soft, about 8 to 10 minutes. Add the sausages. Pour the beer into the skillet. Bring to a boil, reduce the heat to a simmer, partially cover, and steam the sausages for 20 minutes, or until the sausages are cooked through and no longer pink in the center. Remove the sausages to a cutting board and thinly slice.

Add the cooked potatoes and the sliced bratwurst and remaining contents of the skillet to the Dutch oven. Gently simmer until just heated through.

Ladle into individual bowls and garnish each serving with chopped chives and crispy fried bacon.

MARGE'S ARTICHOKE & SAUSAGE SOUP

This recipe was given to me by my friend Marge McDonald. It is adapted from one she cut out of the newspaper years ago and included in a personal cookbook put together for her children. The anise, or licorice, flavor in this soup comes from a variety of sources: the fresh fennel, the fennel seed in the sausage, the Italian seasoning, and the Sambuca. A simple green salad and country-style Italian bread complete this rustic, hearty meal.

Serves 8

1 POUND HOT ITALIAN SAUSAGE

2 POUNDS SWEET OR MILD ITALIAN SAUSAGE

3 LEEKS, CLEANED, TRIMMED, AND THINLY SLICED

2 FENNEL BULBS, HALVED, TOUGH CORE REMOVED, AND CHOPPED (RESERVE THE FENNEL FRONDS AND CHOP FOR GARNISH)

4 GARLIC CLOVES, CHOPPED

2 (28 OUNCE) CANS PLUM TOMATOES WITH THEIR JUICE

2 (14 OUNCE) CANS MARINATED ARTICHOKE HEARTS, DRAINED

1 CUP RED WINE

¼ CUP SAMBUCA (OPTIONAL)

⅓ CUP CHOPPED FRESH BASIL

2 TABLESPOONS FRESH THYME LEAVES

1 TO 2 TABLESPOONS DRIED ITALIAN SEASONING

1 TEASPOON SALT

½ TEASPOON BLACK PEPPER

1 TEASPOON SUGAR

3 CUPS BEEF STOCK, PREFERABLY HOMEMADE

1½ CUPS MEDIUM BARLEY

1 CUP SHAVED PARMESAN CHEESE

Lightly coat a 5½-quart Dutch oven with nonstick cooking spray. Crumble the sausage into the pot. Fry the sausage over medium-high heat until it cooks through and is no longer pink. Drain any excess fat and discard. Return the pot with the sausage to the heat.

Add the leeks, fennel, and garlic to the cooked sausage. Cook until the vegetables begin to wilt, about 5 minutes.

Add the tomatoes with their juice, breaking them with the back of a spoon. Cut the artichokes into thirds and stir into the soup.

Stir in the red wine and Sambuca. Add the basil, thyme leaves, Italian seasoning, salt, pepper, and sugar. Cover and simmer over medium-low heat, stirring occasionally, for 1 hour.

Add the beef stock and barley. Return to a boil, reduce the heat, and simmer, uncovered, until the barley is tender and the soup thickens, about 45 minutes. Remove from the heat.

Let the soup rest for at least 2 hours to allow the flavors to mingle. Skim any fat that accumulates on the top. When ready to serve, reheat and ladle the soup into individual bowls. Garnish each serving with shavings of fresh Parmesan cheese and the reserved chopped fronds of fennel.

NEW ENGLAND CORNED BEEF & CABBAGE SOUP

This is one of those great "clean out the crisper drawer" recipes. Any and all root vegetables work well in this soup. Use what you have on hand or need to use up quickly. The beets add a lovely tinge of color, and the horseradish contributes a bit of bite.

Serves 8

1 (3 TO 4 POUND) CORNED BEEF BRISKET

ABOUT 12 CUPS WATER

8 NEW POTATOES, SCRUBBED AND QUARTERED

1 POUND PEARL ONIONS, PEELED

1 POUND BABY CARROTS, SCRAPED

3 PARSNIPS, PEELED AND SLICED

SALT AND FRESHLY GROUND BLACK PEPPER

½ SMALL HEAD GREEN CABBAGE, HALVED, CORED, AND

    THINLY SLICED (ABOUT 4 CUPS)

1 (16 OUNCE) CAN SLICED BEETS, RINSED AND DRAINED

¼ CUP CHOPPED FRESH PARSLEY

Horseradish Sauce

1 CUP SOUR CREAM

¼ CUP PREPARED HORSERADISH

2 TABLESPOONS DIJON MUSTARD

1 TABLESPOON APPLE CIDER VINEGAR

SALT AND FRESHLY GROUND BLACK PEPPER

Rinse the corned beef under running water and trim off any fat. Place in a 5½-quart Dutch oven. Cover with cold water and bring to a boil, skimming off any scum that rises to the surface. Reduce the heat to low and simmer, covered, for 3½ hours. Remove the meat and allow it to sit for 10 minutes. Cut into 1-inch cubes and return to the cooking broth.

Add the new potatoes, pearl onions, carrots, and parsnips. Cover and simmer for 30 minutes, or until vegetables are tender. Add the sliced cabbage and sliced beets and cook for 15 minutes.

Ladle the soup into bowls and put a dollop of Horseradish Sauce on each serving. Sprinkle with chopped parsley.

Horseradish Sauce
In a medium bowl, combine all ingredients.

MOROCCAN LAMB SOUP WITH COUSCOUS

The wonderful flavors of northern Africa, both sweet and spicy, come alive in this most unusual offering. The ingredient list for this recipe may look somewhat daunting, but the end result is well worth the effort. Serve toasted pita wedges with the soup for an interesting crunch contrast.

Serves 8 to 10

2 TABLESPOONS OLIVE OIL, DIVIDED

2 POUNDS GROUND LAMB

2 TABLESPOONS CHOPPED FRESH GINGER

2 TABLESPOONS CHOPPED FRESH MINT

1 TABLESPOON CHOPPED FRESH ROSEMARY

1 TABLESPOON GROUND CUMIN

½ TEASPOON CAYENNE PEPPER

½ TEASPOON GROUND CINNAMON

1 CUP GOLDEN RAISINS

SALT AND FRESHLY GROUND BLACK PEPPER

1 ONION, HALVED, PEELED, AND THINLY SLICED

4 GARLIC CLOVES, CHOPPED

2 RIBS OF CELERY, THINLY SLICED

1 SMALL EGGPLANT, CUT INTO ½-INCH DICE

1 (28 OUNCE) CAN CRUSHED TOMATOES WITH ADDED PUREE

2 TABLESPOONS CHOPPED CELERY LEAVES

1 TABLESPOON FRESH THYME LEAVES

1 TABLESPOON CHOPPED FRESH OREGANO OR MARJORAM

1 TABLESPOON SUGAR

¼ CUP APPLE CIDER VINEGAR

8 CUPS BEEF STOCK, PREFERABLY HOMEMADE

1 CUP COUSCOUS

1 (15½ OUNCE) CAN CHICKPEAS, RINSED AND DRAINED

½ CUP THINLY SLICED GREEN OLIVES

¼ CUP CAPERS, RINSED AND DRAINED

1 CUP CRUMBLED FETA CHEESE

In a 5½-quart Dutch oven, heat 1 tablespoon of the olive oil until very hot. Add the lamb and cook over medium heat until nicely browned. Drain off any excess fat. Add the ginger, mint, rosemary, cumin, cayenne pepper, cinnamon, raisins, and salt and pepper to taste. Cook over medium heat for 3 to 4 minutes, or until very fragrant, stirring often. Remove to a large bowl and set aside.

Return the pan to the heat and add the remaining tablespoon of olive oil. Add the onion, garlic, and celery and cook over medium-high heat for 5 minutes, or until the vegetables begin to wilt. Add the cubed eggplant and continue cooking until the eggplant begins to soften, about 5 minutes more. Reduce the heat to medium and add the crushed tomatoes, celery leaves, thyme, and oregano or marjoram. Bring to a simmer, reduce the heat to low, cover, and cook for about 30 minutes, stirring occasionally to prevent sticking.

Stir in the sugar, apple cider vinegar, and beef stock. Add the reserved lamb mixture, couscous, and chickpeas. Cook for 8 to 10 minutes. Season to taste with salt and pepper.

In a small bowl, mix together the green olives, capers, and feta cheese. Ladle the soup into individual serving bowls and sprinkle each serving with 2 tablespoons of the olive-cheese mixture. Serve at once.

BRAISED BEEFY VEGETABLE SOUP

Who would ever guess that this wonderfully flavored beefy soup uses only 1 pound of meat to serve eight people? By braising the meat first, success is guaranteed. This soup is a wintertime favorite among my family and friends.

Serves 8

2 TABLESPOONS OLIVE OIL

1 POUND BOTTOM ROUND STEAK, TRIMMED OF ALL VISIBLE
FAT AND CUT INTO 1-INCH CUBES

2 CUPS RED WINE

½ CUP BALSAMIC VINEGAR

¼ CUP COARSE-GRAINED DIJON MUSTARD

2 ONIONS, PEELED AND QUARTERED

1 (16 OUNCE) CAN CHOPPED TOMATOES WITH THEIR JUICE

8 GARLIC CLOVES, THINLY SLICED

8 CUPS BEEF STOCK, PREFERABLY HOMEMADE

3 CARROTS, CUT INTO ½-INCH SLICES

3 RIBS OF CELERY, CUT ON THE DIAGONAL INTO ½-INCH SLICES

2 CUPS SLICED FRESH MUSHROOMS

8 SMALL NEW POTATOES, SCRUBBED AND CUT IN HALF

2 TABLESPOONS CHOPPED FRESH ROSEMARY

2 TABLESPOONS CHOPPED FRESH BASIL

¼ CUP PLUS 2 TABLESPOONS CHOPPED FRESH PARSLEY

SALT AND FRESHLY GROUND BLACK PEPPER

In a 5½-quart Dutch oven, heat the olive oil until sizzling. Add the steak and brown on all sides.

Stir in the red wine, balsamic vinegar, mustard, onions, chopped tomatoes, and garlic. Cover and simmer over low heat for about 2 hours, or until the meat is very tender and falling apart.

Add the beef stock, carrots, celery, mushrooms, new potatoes, rosemary, basil, 2 tablespoons of chopped parsley, and salt and pepper to taste. Bring to a boil, then reduce heat to medium. Cover with a tight-fitting lid and simmer, stirring every 10 minutes or so, for 30 to 40 minutes, or until the vegetables are very tender.

Taste and adjust seasonings with additional salt and pepper if necessary. Sprinkle with remaining chopped parsley just before serving.

FIERY THAI GRILLED BEEF SOUP

A good homemade beef stock is essential in this quick and easy soup (an even easier soup if you have leftover beef). The recipe is based on the traditional beef salad served as an appetizer in many Thai restaurants. This soup adaptation combines the "Four S's" of Thai cuisine: sweet, salty, sour, and spicy.

Serves 8

2 POUNDS BEEF TENDERLOIN, LONDON BROIL, OR SIRLOIN
   STEAK, COOKED VERY RARE AND SLICED VERY THIN

8 GREEN ONIONS, CHOPPED

4 SHALLOTS, CHOPPED

½ CUP TIGHTLY PACKED CILANTRO LEAVES

¼ CUP TIGHTLY PACKED MINT LEAVES

1 TO 2 TEASPOONS RED PEPPER FLAKES

1 TABLESPOON BROWN SUGAR

⅓ CUP FISH SAUCE

½ CUP FRESHLY SQUEEZED LIME JUICE

1 SMALL ENGLISH CUCUMBER, PEELED, HALVED LENGTHWISE,
   SEEDED, AND THINLY SLICED ON THE DIAGONAL

1 CUP CHERRY TOMATOES, HALVED

8 CUPS BEEF STOCK, PREFERABLY HOMEMADE

CILANTRO SPRIGS

In a large glass bowl, combine the sliced beef, green onions, shallots, cilantro, mint, red pepper flakes, brown sugar, fish sauce, lime juice, sliced cucumbers, and cherry tomatoes. Let sit for 15 minutes.

In a 4½-quart Dutch oven, bring the beef stock to a boil. Stir in the marinated meat and vegetables. Remove from the heat. Taste and adjust seasonings, adding additional fish sauce, lime juice, or sugar if desired. Serve at once, garnishing each serving with the sprigs of cilantro.

HEARTY REUBEN SOUP

I first had this satisfying soup at the home of my dear friend and colleague Nathalie Dupree as we were testing recipes for one of her many cookbooks. I have adapted some of the ingredients, but the basic technique remains the same. The seasoning sauce makes the soup taste exactly like the classic Reuben sandwich. It has been the perfect crowd-pleaser for many a Super Bowl party I have hosted.

Serves 8 to 10

1 (3 TO 4 POUND) CORNED BEEF BRISKET

10 CUPS RESERVED COOKING LIQUID FROM BRISKET

1 (16 OUNCE) CAN SAUERKRAUT, RINSED AND DRAINED

4 CUPS THINLY SLICED RED CABBAGE (ABOUT HALF A LARGE
   HEAD, CORED)

1 (12 OUNCE) BOTTLE BEER

2 ONIONS, HALVED, PEELED, AND THINLY SLICED

4 GARLIC CLOVES, CHOPPED

¼ CUP DIJON MUSTARD

4 TABLESPOONS BUTTER

¼ CUP FLOUR

3 TABLESPOONS TOMATO PASTE

1 TABLESPOON PAPRIKA

2 TO 3 TEASPOONS CARAWAY SEED, SLIGHTLY CRUSHED

SALT AND FRESHLY GROUND BLACK PEPPER

12 SLICES DARK PUMPERNICKEL BREAD, CUBED AND
   BAKED FOR 10 MINUTES AT 350°F

2 CUPS SHREDDED SWISS CHEESE

Rinse the corned beef under running water and place in a 5-quart Dutch oven. Cover with cold water and bring to a boil, skimming off any scum that rises to the surface. Reduce the heat to low and simmer, covered, for 3½ hours. Remove the meat from the hot liquid and allow to cool. Trim away any fat, then cut the brisket into 1-inch cubes. Set aside.

Measure out 10 cups of the cooking liquid and discard the remainder. Set aside 2 cups of the liquid and put the remaining 8 cups back into the Dutch oven. Bring to a boil. Add the sauerkraut, cabbage, beer, onions, garlic, and Dijon mustard. Bring to a boil, reduce heat, and simmer for 15 to 20 minutes, or until the cabbage is tender.

Meanwhile, make the seasoning sauce. In a large skillet, melt the butter, then stir in the flour. Cook over medium heat for 2 to 3 minutes, or until the flour is a light tan color. Stir in the tomato paste then the reserved 2 cups of cooking liquid. Stir in the paprika, caraway seed, and salt and pepper to taste. Continue stirring until the mixture thickens.

Transfer the seasoning sauce to the soup pot and add the cubed corned beef. Cook about 5 minutes, or until heated through. Serve in individual bowls, garnished with pumpernickel croutons and shredded Swiss cheese.

GREEK MEATBALL SOUP WITH FETA & CUCUMBERS

This meatball soup appeals to kids as well as grownups. The ouzo can be omitted if desired. In that case, substitute ½ teaspoon of crushed anise or fennel seed.

Serves 8

2 POUNDS GROUND LAMB

1 LARGE ONION, FINELY CHOPPED

6 GARLIC CLOVES, FINELY CHOPPED

1 GREEN PEPPER, SEEDED AND FINELY CHOPPED

2 TABLESPOONS OUZO (GREEK ANISE-FLAVORED LIQUEUR)

2 EGGS

1 CUP SEASONED BREAD CRUMBS

3 TABLESPOONS CHOPPED FRESH MINT, DIVIDED

1 TABLESPOON CHOPPED FRESH DILL

1 TABLESPOON CHOPPED FRESH ROSEMARY

1 TEASPOON GROUND CUMIN

½ TO 1 TEASPOON CAYENNE PEPPER

SALT AND FRESHLY GROUND BLACK PEPPER

8 CUPS CHICKEN STOCK, PREFERABLY HOMEMADE

JUICE OF 2 LEMONS

2 CUCUMBERS, PEELED, HALVED LENTHWISE, SEEDED, AND
    THINLY SLICED

1 CUP HALVED CHERRY TOMATOES

1 CUP CRUMBLED FETA CHEESE

In a large bowl, combine the ground lamb, onion, garlic, green pepper, ouzo, eggs, bread crumbs, 1 tablespoon of the chopped mint, dill, rosemary, cumin, cayenne pepper, and salt and pepper to taste. Shape the mixture into 1-inch meatballs and place on a broiler pan that has been sprayed with a nonstick cooking spray. Cover with foil and refrigerate for about 30 minutes.

Preheat the oven to 450°F. Place the meatballs in the oven and bake for about 20 minutes, removing the foil after 10 minutes.

In a 4½-quart Dutch oven, bring the chicken stock to a boil. Stir in the remaining 2 tablespoons of chopped mint, lemon juice, cucumbers, cherry tomatoes, and cooked meatballs. Simmer gently for 3 to 5 minutes, or until the cucumbers are crisp-tender.

Ladle into individual bowls and top each serving with feta cheese. Serve with pita bread cut into wedges.

CREAMY BEEF STROGANOFF NOODLE SOUP

Beef stroganoff is named in honor of the 19th-century Russian diplomat, Count Paul Stroganov. This thick and creamy soup is elegant enough to be served on white linen, yet it also manages to evoke that comfort food feeling that makes it suitable for TV trays in the family room.

Serves 8 to 10

2 POUNDS VERY LEAN BONELESS SIRLOIN STEAK, THINLY SLICED

SALT AND FRESHLY GROUND BLACK PEPPER

1 CUP RED WINE OR WATER

1 OUNCE DRIED MUSHROOMS

2 TABLESPOONS OLIVE OIL

1 RED ONION, CHOPPED

1 RED PEPPER, SEEDED AND THINLY SLICED

2 CARROTS, SHREDDED

4 GARLIC CLOVES, CHOPPED

3 CUPS SLICED FRESH MUSHROOMS

4 TABLESPOONS BUTTER

¼ CUP FLOUR

10 CUPS CHICKEN OR BEEF STOCK, PREFERABLY HOMEMADE

2 TABLESPOONS WORCESTERSHIRE SAUCE

1 TABLESPOON DRY MUSTARD

1 TABLESPOON DRIED ITALIAN SEASONING

1 (16 OUNCE) CONTAINER SOUR CREAM

1 (12 OUNCE) PACKAGE COOKED EGG NOODLES

4 GREEN ONIONS, CHOPPED

3 HARD-COOKED EGGS, PEELED AND CHOPPED

Lightly season the sliced steak with salt and pepper. In a medium glass bowl, combine the red wine or water and dried mushrooms and let sit for 1 hour.

Coat the bottom of a 5½-quart Dutch oven with the olive oil. Add the steak, red onion, red pepper, carrots, garlic, and fresh mushrooms. Cook over medium heat until the steak is browned and the vegetables are tender, about 15 minutes.

Stir in the reconstituted mushrooms with their liquid and cook for 5 minutes. Remove the contents of the pan, including the juices, to a large bowl and set aside.

Wipe the Dutch oven dry with a paper towel and return to the stove. Over medium heat, melt the butter and add the flour, stirring constantly until you have a light tan roux, about 2 minutes.

Add 8 cups of the stock and cook until the mixture reduces by one-third, about 10 minutes. In a food processor or blender, combine the Worcestershire sauce, dry mustard, Italian seasoning, and sour cream. Process until smooth. Add this to the reduced stock and stir constantly, until it just comes to a boil. Stir in the reserved meat-vegetable mixture and the egg noodles. Add more chicken or beef stock (up to 2 cups) if the soup is too thick. Cook until just heated through, 2 to 3 minutes. Taste, adding salt and pepper if necessary.

Ladle into a soup tureen or individual bowls and sprinkle with green onions and chopped egg. Serve at once.

FLORENTINE SAUSAGE & PEPPERONI SOUP

Ever had pizza in a bowl? This soup combines all the flavors of that wonderful slice of life. It is perfect for teenagers after a Friday-night football game, or as supper at a holiday tree-trimming party for family and friends. When I freeze this soup, I don't add the grated cheeses or bread crumbs until I'm ready to reheat the soup.

Serves 8

2 TABLESPOONS OLIVE OIL

1 POUND HOT ITALIAN SAUSAGE

24 LARGE MUSHROOMS, STEMS REMOVED AND THINLY SLICED

1 (28 OUNCE) CAN CHOPPED TOMATOES WITH THEIR JUICE

½ POUND PEPPERONI, THINLY SLICED AND EACH SLICE CUT
   IN HALF

4 GARLIC CLOVES, CHOPPED

6 GREEN ONIONS, CHOPPED

2 TABLESPOONS TOMATO PASTE

2 TABLESPOONS CHOPPED FRESH OREGANO

2 TABLESPOONS CHOPPED FRESH ROSEMARY

2 TABLESPOONS CAPERS, RINSED AND DRAINED

1 TABLESPOON ANCHOVY PASTE

8 CUPS BEEF STOCK, PREFERABLY HOMEMADE

2 (10 OUNCE) PACKAGES FROZEN CHOPPED SPINACH,
   DEFROSTED AND SQUEEZED DRY

SALT AND FRESHLY GROUND BLACK PEPPER

½ CUP GRATED PARMESAN CHEESE

½ CUP GRATED ROMANO CHEESE

½ CUP SEASONED BREAD CRUMBS

1 CUP SHREDDED MOZZARELLA CHEESE

In a 5½-quart Dutch oven, heat the olive oil until sizzling. Crumble the sausage into the pot and cook over medium-high heat, stirring to break up the larger pieces, about 8 minutes, or until cooked through and no longer pink. Drain off any excess fat.

Stir in the mushrooms, tomatoes, pepperoni, garlic, green onions, tomato paste, oregano, rosemary, capers, and anchovy paste. Bring to a boil, reduce the heat to a simmer, and cook until thickened, stirring often, about 10 minutes.

Add the beef stock, chopped spinach, and salt and pepper to taste. Simmer for 15 minutes, or until slightly thickened.

Just before serving, stir in the Parmesan cheese, Romano cheese, and bread crumbs.

Preheat the oven to 400°F. Ladle the soup into individual heat-proof bowls. Top each serving with some of the mozzarella cheese and bake until the cheese melts and the soup is bubbly, about 5 to 7 minutes. Serve at once.

CUBAN PORK & MUSTARD GREEN SOUP

The addition of orange zest gives a bright, citrus sweetness to the savory flavor of this old Cuban dish. Hot Italian sausage can be substituted if Spanish chorizo is unavailable in your area. Allspice, also known as Jamaican pepper, is a small, brown berry so named because it combines the tastes of cinnamon, nutmeg, and cloves. You can substitute kale, turnip, or spinach for the mustard greens if you like.

Serves 8

2 POUNDS LEAN, BONELESS PORK LOIN, CUT INTO 1-INCH CUBES

1 POUND CHORIZO SAUSAGE, CASINGS REMOVED, CRUMBLED

3 ONIONS, CHOPPED

4 GARLIC CLOVES, CHOPPED

1 CUP DRIED BROWN LENTILS, PICKED OVER

10 CUPS CHICKEN STOCK, PREFERABLY HOMEMADE

1 (8 OUNCE) CAN TOMATO PUREE

2 TABLESPOONS CHOPPED FRESH MARJORAM

2 TEASPOONS GROUND CUMIN

½ TEASPOON ALLSPICE

SALT AND FRESHLY GROUND BLACK PEPPER

4 CARROTS, CUT INTO ¼-INCH SLICES

3 RIBS OF CELERY, CUT INTO ¼-INCH SLICES

2 SWEET POTATOES, CUT INTO ¼-INCH SLICES

1½ POUNDS MUSTARD GREENS, WASHED, STEMMED, AND TORN INTO LARGE PIECES

FINELY GRATED ZEST OF 2 ORANGES

In a 5½-quart Dutch oven over medium-high heat, combine the pork cubes, crumbled chorizo, onions, garlic, dried lentils, chicken stock, tomato puree, marjoram, cumin, allspice, and salt and pepper to taste. Bring to a boil, reduce the heat to medium, cover, and cook for 1 hour. Skim away any excess fat that accumulates at the top of the soup.

Stir in the carrots, celery, and sweet potatoes. Cover and simmer for 30 minutes, or until the vegetables are tender.

Stir in the mustard greens. Cook for 10 minutes, or until the greens are tender and the soup is nicely thickened. Add the orange zest and simmer for 5 minutes. Adjust the seasonings with additional salt and pepper if needed. Serve hot.

SOUTHWESTERN PINTO BEAN SOUP

All the tastes of a traditional chili come through in the form of a soup in this mouth-watering meal in a bowl. For a little more regional authenticity, substitute cranberry or rattlesnake beans for the pintos. Icy-cold beer and jalapeño cornsticks are perfect accompaniments to this soup.

Serves 8 to 10

2 TABLESPOONS VEGETABLE OIL

3 ONIONS, HALVED, PEELED, AND THINLY SLICED

6 GARLIC CLOVES, CHOPPED

2 GREEN PEPPERS, SEEDED AND THINLY SLICED

2 TABLESPOONS CHILI POWDER

1 TABLESPOON GROUND CUMIN

1 TEASPOON RED PEPPER FLAKES

SALT AND FRESHLY GROUND BLACK PEPPER

1 POUND DRIED PINTO BEANS, PRESOAKED (SEE PAGE 9)

6 CUPS BEEF STOCK, PREFERABLY HOMEMADE

6 CUPS WATER

2 SMOKED HAM HOCKS

2 BAY LEAVES, CRUMBLED

2 POUNDS SLICED KIELBASA SAUSAGE

1 (28 OUNCE) CAN CHOPPED TOMATOES WITH THEIR JUICE

2 (8 OUNCE) CAN RED ENCHILADA SAUCE

¼ CUP FRESHLY SQUEEZED LIME JUICE

½ CUP CHOPPED FRESH CILANTRO

In a 5½-quart Dutch oven, heat the oil over medium-high heat. Add the onions, garlic, and green peppers and cook for 10 minutes, or until the vegetables soften.

Stir in the chili powder, cumin, red pepper flakes, and salt and pepper to taste. Cook for 2 minutes. Add the drained pintos, along with the beef stock, water, ham hocks, and bay leaves. Reduce the heat, partially cover, and simmer the soup for 2 hours.

Remove the ham hocks. When they are cool enough to handle, remove the meat from the bones. Set the meat aside and discard the bones.

To the simmering soup, stir in the kielbasa, tomatoes, and enchilada sauce. Simmer, partially covered, for 30 minutes.

Stir in the lime juice, cilantro, and reserved ham meat. Serve at once.

IRISH BEEF, CABBAGE & BARLEY SOUP

If I had a choice between a pot of gold at the end of the rainbow or a pot of this meat and braised vegetable medley, which would I choose? Let me have another bowl of soup and then I'll decide. Traditional Irish soda bread would round out this meal very nicely.

Serves 8

2 TABLESPOONS PEANUT OIL

1 (3½ POUND) CHUCK ROAST, TRIMMED OF VISIBLE FAT
AND CUT INTO 1-INCH CHUNKS

1 TEASPOON SALT

½ TEASPOON BLACK PEPPER

2 ONIONS, CHOPPED

6 GARLIC CLOVES, CHOPPED

2 PARSNIPS, PEELED AND CUT INTO ½-INCH DICE

2 TURNIPS, PEELED AND CUT INTO ½-INCH DICE

½ HEAD SMALL GREEN CABBAGE, CUT INTO 1-INCH CHUNKS
(ABOUT 4 CUPS)

1 (16 OUNCE) CAN STEWED TOMATOES WITH THEIR JUICE

⅔ CUP DRIED SPLIT PEAS

⅔ CUP MEDIUM PEARL BARLEY, RINSED AND DRAINED

10 CUPS BEEF STOCK, PREFERABLY HOMEMADE

½ TEASPOON CARAWAY SEEDS

In a 5½-quart Dutch oven, heat the peanut oil until sizzling. Lightly season the chuck roast with salt and pepper. Place the meat in the Dutch oven and cook over medium-high heat until the meat is browned and seared on all sides. Remove from the pot and set aside.

To the drippings in the pot, add the onions, garlic, parsnips, turnips, and cabbage. Cook the vegetables until they begin to lightly brown, about 15 minutes. Return the meat to the pan.

Add the stewed tomatoes, split peas, barley, beef stock, and caraway seeds. Simmer over low heat, covered, for 2 to 3 hours. Be sure to check the soup every now and then and stir to prevent sticking. Adjust seasonings with additional salt and pepper if needed.

GREEK MOUSSAKA SOUP

Sometimes eggplant can have a bitter edge. To alleviate this problem, place the cubed eggplant in a colander and sprinkle with ¼ cup kosher salt. Place in the sink and let sit for 30 minutes. The salt will draw out the bitter juices. Rinse very well under cold running water and pat the eggplant dry before tossing with the flour and continuing with the recipe.
A crisp green salad, soft pita bread, and a jug of Chianti—dinner is complete.

Serves 8

2 POUNDS GROUND LAMB

2 ONIONS, CHOPPED

1 RED PEPPER, SEEDED AND CHOPPED

2 CUPS SLICED MUSHROOMS

3 GARLIC CLOVES, CHOPPED

2 TABLESPOONS OLIVE OIL

1 MEDIUM EGGPLANT, CUBED

3 TABLESPOONS FLOUR

6 CUPS CHICKEN STOCK, PREFERABLY HOMEMADE

1 (28 OUNCE) CAN CHOPPED TOMATOES WITH THEIR JUICE

¼ CUP TOMATO PASTE

2 TABLESPOONS CHOPPED FRESH OREGANO

1 TABLESPOON CHOPPED FRESH MINT

1 TABLESPOON CHOPPED FRESH ROSEMARY

1 TEASPOON RED PEPPER FLAKES

¼ TEASPOON GROUND CINNAMON

¼ CUP SHERRY VINEGAR

1 TABLESPOON SUGAR

SALT AND FRESHLY GROUND BLACK PEPPER

2 CUPS COOKED EGG NOODLES

1 (8 OUNCE) CONTAINER SOUR CREAM

1 CUP HALF AND HALF

½ CUP FRESHLY GRATED PARMESAN CHEESE

FRESHLY GRATED NUTMEG

1 CUP CRUMBLED FETA CHEESE

2 TABLESPOONS CHOPPED FRESH MINT

In a 5½-quart Dutch oven over medium-high heat, combine the lamb, onions, red pepper, mushrooms, and garlic. Cook until the meat is browned and the vegetables are soft. Drain off any excess fat and transfer the contents to a large bowl.

In the same pot, heat the olive oil over medium-high heat. Toss the cubed eggplant with the flour and then add to the pot. Cook for 6 to 8 minutes, or until eggplant begins to brown. Return the meat mixture to the pot. Stir in the chicken stock, chopped tomatoes, tomato paste, oregano, mint, rosemary, red pepper flakes, cinnamon, sherry vinegar, and sugar. Season to taste with salt and pepper. Bring to a boil, reduce the heat, and simmer, covered, for 30 minutes.

Stir in the cooked egg noodles, sour cream, half and half, Parmesan cheese, and a sprinkling of nutmeg. Bring to just below a boil. Ladle into individual serving bowls and garnish each serving with the feta cheese and chopped mint.

MARINATED STEAK & POTATO SOUP

This recipe is adapted from one in Lee Bailey's Soup Meals. *The Asian accents in the marinade subtly flavor this thick and hearty soup.*

Serves 8

⅓ CUP DRY SHERRY

3 TABLESPOONS HOISIN SAUCE

3 TABLESPOONS FRESHLY SQUEEZED LEMON JUICE

2 TABLESPOONS SOY SAUCE

1 TABLESPOON CHOPPED GINGER

1 GARLIC CLOVE, CHOPPED

2 POUNDS THICK SIRLOIN STEAK, TRIMMED AND CUT INTO
   1-INCH CUBES

3 TABLESPOONS OLIVE OIL

3 ONIONS, HALVED, PEELED, AND THINLY SLICED

3 CARROTS, COARSELY CHOPPED

3 RIBS OF CELERY, FINELY CHOPPED

1 POUND FRESH BUTTON MUSHROOMS, THINLY SLICED

3 TABLESPOONS BUTTER

1 TABLESPOON PEANUT OIL

FLOUR FOR DUSTING

10 CUPS BEEF STOCK, PREFERABLY HOMEMADE

2 POTATOES, PEELED AND CUT INTO 1-INCH CUBES

1 TABLESPOON WORCESTERSHIRE SAUCE

¼ CUP TOMATO PASTE

SALT AND FRESHLY GROUND BLACK PEPPER

1 BAY LEAF, CRUMBLED

½ CUP MEDIUM PEARL BARLEY, RINSED AND DRAINED

1 (10 OUNCE) PACKAGE PREWASHED SPINACH LEAVES,
   STEMS REMOVED

In a large bowl, whisk together the dry sherry, Hoisin sauce, lemon juice, soy sauce, ginger, and garlic. Stir in the sirloin cubes, cover, and marinate at room temperature for 1 hour.

Meanwhile, heat the olive oil in a 5½-quart Dutch oven. Add the onions, carrots, and celery. Cook over medium-high heat for about 5 minutes. Stir in the mushrooms and cook until they are just wilted, about 5 minutes. With a slotted spoon, remove the vegetables from the pot and set aside.

Add the butter and peanut oil to the pot and heat over medium-high heat. Pat the steak cubes dry and dust them with flour, shaking off the excess. Brown the meat, stirring occasionally to prevent the flour from burning. Add the beef stock, potatoes, Worcestershire sauce, tomato paste, salt and pepper to taste, bay leaf, and barley. Bring to a boil, reduce the heat, cover, and simmer, stirring occasionally, for 15 minutes.

Add the reserved vegetables, cover, and continue cooking until the barley is soft, about 20 minutes. Remove the pot from the heat, stir in the spinach, cover the pot once again, and let sit for about 5 to 6 minutes. Stir and taste for seasonings, adding salt and pepper as needed. Serve at once.

SEAFOOD SOUPS

Roasted Plum Tomato and Salmon Soup

Creamy Crab and Cremini Mushroom Soup

Wine-Braised Cream of Mussel Soup

Nouvelle Noel Soup

Tuscan Shrimp and Cannellini Bean Soup

Southern Seafood Gumbo

Jamaican-Style Crab Chowder with Black Beans

New England Clam Chowder

Manhattan-Style Clam Chowder

Seafood Dumpling Soup with Gremolata

Succotash Soup with Baby Shrimp

Classic Lobster Bisque

Oysters Rockefeller Chowder

Dixieland Cioppino

Fresh and Salted Codfish Chowder

Smoked Trout Chowder

Penne Pasta and Smoked Salmon Soup with Tomatoes,

Peppered Vodka, and Cream

ROASTED PLUM TOMATO & SALMON SOUP

Even in the dead of winter, you can usually find ripe plum tomatoes for this soup. Roasting the tomatoes lends a delicate, smoky taste to the finished soup. Catfish, flounder, or tilapia can be substituted for the salmon, although the taste will not be as rich.

Serves 6 to 8

4 POUNDS RIPE PLUM TOMATOES, HALVED LENGTHWISE

3 TABLESPOONS BUTTER

1 RED ONION, FINELY CHOPPED

2 RIBS OF CELERY, THINLY SLICED

2 CARROTS, SHREDDED

3 GARLIC CLOVES, CHOPPED

8 CUPS CHICKEN STOCK, PREFERABLY HOMEMADE

2 TABLESPOONS CHOPPED FRESH PARSLEY

1 TABLESPOON CHOPPED FRESH TARRAGON

¼ CUP MEDIUM BARLEY

SALT AND FRESHLY GROUND BLACK PEPPER

2 POUNDS SKINLESS SALMON FILLETS, CUT INTO
  1-INCH CHUNKS

½ CUP DRY WHITE WINE

1 TABLESPOON FRESHLY SQUEEZED LEMON JUICE

Preheat the broiler. Line a baking sheet with aluminum foil. Place the tomato halves, skin side up, on the prepared pan. Roast about 6 inches from the heat source until the skins are charred and blackened, about 8 to 10 minutes. Remove from the oven and, when cool enough to handle, slip off the skins and gently squeeze the tomatoes to dislodge the seeds. Coarsely chop the tomatoes and set aside.

Melt the butter in a 4½-quart Dutch oven. Add the red onion, celery, carrots, and garlic and cook over medium-high heat until the onion begins to wilt, about 5 minutes. Stir in the roasted tomatoes. Add the chicken stock. Simmer, uncovered, for 15 minutes.

Stir in the parsley, tarragon, and barley. Cover and cook for an additional 20 to 25 minutes, or until the barley is tender. Season to taste with salt and pepper.

Remove the lid and stir in the salmon, white wine, and lemon juice. Simmer for 5 to 8 minutes, or until the fish flakes easily with a fork. Serve at once.

CREAMY CRAB & CREMINI MUSHROOM SOUP

Let this simple yet elegant soup set the mood for your next festive dinner party. You can find pasteurized crab meat packed in 8-ounce tins on ice in the seafood display of most grocery stores. Sometimes these cans will contain bright coral-colored roe (eggs). Consider this a bonus, as the roe adds a delicate sweetness to the creamy soup.

Serves 4 to 6

8 TABLESPOONS (1 STICK) BUTTER, DIVIDED

1 POUND CREMINI MUSHROOMS, THINLY SLICED

½ CUP DRY WHITE WINE

1½ CUPS FRESHLY GRATED PARMESAN CHEESE

1 POUND PASTEURIZED LUMP CRAB MEAT, PICKED OVER
  FOR SHELLS

5 TABLESPOONS FLOUR

6 CUPS FISH OR CHICKEN STOCK, PREFERABLY HOMEMADE

2 CUPS HEAVY CREAM

SALT AND WHITE PEPPER

¼ CUP DRY SHERRY

¼ CUP CHOPPED FRESH PARSLEY

In a 12-inch skillet, melt 3 tablespoons of the butter until sizzling hot. Add the mushrooms and cook, stirring often, over medium-high heat until the mushrooms begin to wilt, about 3 minutes. Stir in the white wine and cook until the wine has completely reduced, about 5 minutes. Stir in the Parmesan cheese and the crab meat. Sauté for 2 minutes and set aside.

In a 4½-quart Dutch oven, melt the remaining 5 tablespoons of butter over medium heat. Stir in the flour and cook for 2 minutes, or until the flour just begins to turn a light straw color. Add the fish or chicken stock and cream, whisking constantly. As the soup begins to thicken, stir in the mushroom and crab mixture. Season to taste with salt and white pepper.

Just before serving, stir in the dry sherry and chopped parsley.

WINE-BRAISED CREAM OF MUSSEL SOUP

Mussels can vary considerably in their saltiness and grittiness, depending on their source. To clean, place them in a sink with lukewarm water. With your hand, swish the mussels throughout the water, or use a stiff brush to scrub them. Drain and repeat with clean water until no more dirt or grit appears at the bottom of the sink. With a sharp knife, remove any barnacles and, with your hands, pull the beards away from the shells. (The beard is a small, fibrous mass that the mussel uses to attach itself to a secure place in the ocean. If you don't see anything that looks like a beard, it probably was already removed by the fishmonger.)

Serves 4

48 SMALL MUSSELS (ABOUT 3 POUNDS), RINSED AND
    DEBEARDED (SEE ABOVE)

1½ CUPS DRY WHITE WINE

1 ONION, HALVED, PEELED, AND THINLY SLICED

2 CARROTS, SHREDDED

2 TOMATOES, SEEDED AND CHOPPED

2 JALAPEÑO PEPPERS, SEEDED AND CHOPPED

1 LEMON, CUT INTO QUARTERS

⅔ CUP ASSORTED CHOPPED FRESH HERBS (PARSLEY, BASIL,
    THYME LEAVES, TARRAGON, AND OREGANO)

SALT AND FRESHLY GROUND BLACK PEPPER

4 CUPS HEAVY CREAM

Parmesan Garlic Croûtes

8 SLICES OF DAY-OLD FRENCH BREAD

¼ CUP OLIVE OIL

2 GARLIC CLOVES, FINELY CHOPPED

¼ CUP FRESHLY GRATED PARMESAN CHEESE

½ TEASPOON RED PEPPER FLAKES

Place the mussels in an 8-quart stockpot with a tight-fitting lid. Add the white wine, onion, carrots, tomatoes, jalapeño peppers, and lemon. Stir in the chopped herbs and salt and pepper to taste.

Cover the stockpot and bring to a boil. Reduce the heat and simmer for approximately 5 to 8 minutes, or until the mussels open. Discard any mussels that did not open. Strain the mussels, reserving the broth and the cooked vegetables. Reserve 12 mussels in the shell for garnish and set aside.

Carefully remove the remaining mussels from the shell and discard the shells. Rinse the pot. Remove the lemon quarters from the strained vegetables and return the vegetables and the steamed mussels to the stockpot. Strain the mussel broth through a triple thickness of cheesecloth to remove any sand or grit. Add the strained broth and the cream to the pot. Bring to a boil. Season to taste with additional salt and pepper.

Ladle the soup into individual bowls and garnish each bowl with three of the mussels in the shell. Serve with Parmesan Garlic Croûtes.

Parmesan Garlic Croûtes

Preheat the broiler. Place the slices of French bread on a baking sheet. In a small bowl, whisk together the remaining ingredients. Brush each piece of bread with this mixture. Broil for 1 to 2 minutes, or until the edges just begin to brown.

NOUVELLE NOEL SOUP

If your family is like mine, it's hard to sneak in new recipes for the holidays. To conjure up the proper nostalgia each year, everything must remain how it was remembered in childhood—including the food. But several years ago, I introduced my family to this soup, adapted from John Hadamuscin's wonderful book The Holidays, *and I succeeded in creating a new and welcome holiday tradition.*

Serves 8

4 TABLESPOONS BUTTER

4 GARLIC CLOVES, THINLY SLICED

2 ONIONS, CHOPPED

6 LEEKS, CLEANED, TRIMMED, AND THINLY SLICED

2 TEASPOONS CURRY POWDER, PREFERABLY MADRAS

2 POUNDS BAY SCALLOPS, RINSED WELL AND PATTED DRY

3 CUPS CHICKEN STOCK, PREFERABLY HOMEMADE

4 EGG YOLKS, LIGHTLY BEATEN

1½ CUPS HEAVY CREAM

2½ CUPS MILK

¼ CUP DRY SHERRY

SALT AND WHITE PEPPER

SNIPPED FRESH CHIVES

TABASCO

PAPRIKA

In a 4½-quart Dutch oven, melt the butter and add the garlic, onions, leeks, and curry powder. Cook over medium heat for about 15 minutes, or until the onions are translucent and tender.

Stir in the scallops and the chicken stock. Bring to a boil, reduce to a simmer, and cook about 10 minutes, or until the scallops are snow-white and opaque. Pour the soup through a strainer into a large bowl. Return the liquid to the pot and keep at a low temperature. Puree the solids in a food processor until very finely ground, adding a little broth as needed to make a fine puree. Return the pureed mixture to the broth.

In a medium bowl, whisk together the egg yolks, cream, and milk. Slowly stir this into the soup mixture over low heat. Continue stirring until thickened and heated through. Bring to just below a boil. Stir in the sherry. Season to taste with salt and white pepper. Serve the soup hot, garnished with snipped chives, Tabasco, and a dash of paprika.

TUSCAN SHRIMP & CANNELLINI BEAN SOUP

Grappa is a colorless, high-alcohol distillation, made from the residue of grape skins and seeds left in the wine press after the juice has been removed. In this recipe, the alcohol from the grappa is allowed to completely evaporate, helping to bind the flavors of the shrimp, garlic, and herbs before the chicken stock is added.

Serves 8

2 (16 OUNCE) CANS WHITE CANNELLINI BEANS, RINSED AND
    DRAINED

1 POUND RIPE PLUM TOMATOES, SEEDED AND VERY COARSELY
    CHOPPED

2 TABLESPOONS CHOPPED FRESH OREGANO

¼ CUP OLIVE OIL

4 TABLESPOONS BUTTER

3 WHOLE, DRIED RED HOT CHILE PEPPERS, OR ½ TEASPOON
    RED PEPPER FLAKES

8 GARLIC CLOVES, CHOPPED

2 BAY LEAVES, CRUMBLED

3 TABLESPOONS CHOPPED FRESH PARSLEY

2 POUNDS LARGE SHRIMP, PEELED AND DEVEINED

2 TABLESPOONS GRAPPA OR DRY VERMOUTH

8 CUPS CHICKEN STOCK, PREFERABLY HOMEMADE

½ CUP THINLY SLICED BASIL LEAVES

SALT AND FRESHLY GROUND BLACK PEPPER

1 CUP SHAVED PARMESAN CHEESE

½ CUP PINE NUTS, LIGHTLY TOASTED (SEE PAGE 13)

BASIL SPRIGS

In a large bowl, combine the cannellini beans, plum tomatoes, and oregano. Toss lightly and set aside.

In a 4½-quart Dutch oven, combine the olive oil and butter and heat until the butter has melted. Add the dried chiles or red pepper flakes and cook over medium heat for 1 minute. Stir in the garlic, bay leaves, parsley, and shrimp and continue to cook until the shrimp just begin to curl, about 2 to 3 minutes. Stir in the grappa or vermouth. Cook for 1 minute. Remove the dried chiles and discard.

Stir in the chicken stock and the bean and tomato mixture. Continue to cook until the soup is just heated through and the shrimp have turned pink. Stir in the basil and salt and pepper to taste.

Ladle into a soup tureen or individual bowls and top each serving with shaved Parmesan cheese and pine nuts. Garnish with fresh sprigs of basil. Serve at once with crusty Italian bread.

SOUTHERN SEAFOOD GUMBO

The word "gumbo" comes from the African word for okra, often used as a thickener for soups and stews. The secret to a good gumbo is toasting the flour in the oil to create a rich, dark, deeply flavored roux. Gumbo filé or filé powder is the name for ground sassafras leaves; it is a wonderful flavor enhancer when sprinkled on the finished dish. Gumbo filé is available in the spice sections of most grocery stores. In the South you sometimes find it on display in the seafood section, among assorted shellfish and crab boil seasonings.

Serves 8 to 10

½ CUP VEGETABLE OIL

½ CUP FLOUR

6 RIBS OF CELERY, CHOPPED

3 ONIONS, CHOPPED

2 GREEN PEPPERS, SEEDED AND CHOPPED

3 GARLIC CLOVES, CHOPPED

1 POUND OKRA, SLICED

10 CUPS CHICKEN STOCK, PREFERABLY HOMEMADE

¼ CUP WORCESTERSHIRE SAUCE

2 TEASPOONS TABASCO

½ CUP CHILI SAUCE OR KETCHUP

1 SMOKED HAM HOCK

SALT AND FRESHLY GROUND BLACK PEPPER

1 BAY LEAF, CRUMBLED

1 TABLESPOON FRESH THYME LEAVES

2 TEASPOONS CHOPPED FRESH ROSEMARY

¼ TEASPOON RED PEPPER FLAKES

2 POUNDS ANDOUILLE OR KIELBASA SAUSAGE, SLICED

1 POUND LARGE SHRIMP, PEELED AND DEVEINED

1 POUND CLAW CRABMEAT, PICKED OVER FOR SHELLS, OR 1
    POUND CRAYFISH TAILS, PEELED

½ CUP CHOPPED FRESH PARSLEY

4 TO 6 CUPS HOT COOKED RICE

GUMBO FILÉ

ADDITIONAL TABASCO

In a heavy 8-quart stockpot, combine the oil and the flour and cook over medium heat, stirring constantly, until the roux is a dark caramel color, about 20 minutes. Be very careful not to burn the roux, or a scorched taste will pervade the gumbo.

Add the celery, onions, green peppers, and garlic and cook for an additional 20 minutes, stirring occasionally. Stir in the okra and cook for 3 minutes. (At this stage the mixture can be cooled, packed in a zip-top freezer bag, and refrigerated or frozen for later use.)

Add the chicken stock, Worcestershire sauce, Tabasco, chili sauce or ketchup, ham hock, salt and pepper to taste, bay leaf, thyme leaves, rosemary, and red pepper flakes. Bring the mixture to a boil, reduce the heat to a simmer, cover, and cook for 1 hour, stirring occasionally.

Add the andouille or kielbasa sausage and cook, uncovered, for 30 minutes longer.

Stir in the shrimp, crabmeat or crayfish tails, and parsley and cook until shrimp begin to curl and turn pink, about 10 minutes.

Remove the ham hock. When cool enough to handle, shred the ham hock meat, discarding the fat and the bone. Stir the shredded meat into the gumbo.

Divide the rice among individual serving bowls. Top with gumbo. Sprinkle with gumbo filé and serve at once. Pass additional Tabasco separately.

JAMAICAN-STYLE CRAB CHOWDER WITH BLACK BEANS

This hearty chowder combines the flavors of sweet crab, fresh vegetables, and the distinctive, spicy-with-sweet taste of jerk seasoning. This special blend of sugar, herbs, and spices (most notably, cayenne pepper, thyme, and allspice) is available in most spice sections of larger supermarkets today. Look for other catch phrases describing jerk seasoning, including Caribbean and Island Magic. Do not overcook the vegetables in this soup. To retain their fresh flavor, they must remain somewhat crisp.

Serves 8

6 STRIPS OF BACON, CUT INTO ½-INCH PIECES

2 ONIONS, CHOPPED

8 GARLIC CLOVES, THINLY SLICED

1 LARGE SWEET POTATO, PEELED AND CUT INTO ½-INCH PIECES

2 RED PEPPERS, SEEDED AND CHOPPED

2 SCOTCH BONNET OR JALAPEÑO PEPPERS, SEEDED AND CHOPPED

7 CUPS VEGETABLE OR CHICKEN STOCK, PREFERABLY HOMEMADE

6 TABLESPOONS CHOPPED FRESH CILANTRO, DIVIDED

2 ZUCCHINI, HALVED LENGTHWISE AND CUT INTO ½-INCH SLICES

2 CUPS FRESH CORN KERNELS (ABOUT 4 EARS)

4 PLUM TOMATOES, SEEDED AND CHOPPED

1 TABLESPOON GROUND CUMIN

1 TABLESPOON JERK SEASONING

2 TEASPOONS CHILI POWDER

SALT AND FRESHLY GROUND BLACK PEPPER

1 CUP MILK MIXED WITH 1 TABLESPOON CORNSTARCH

½ TO 1 TEASPOON TABASCO

1 (15½ OUNCE) CAN BLACK BEANS, RINSED AND DRAINED

1 POUND PASTEURIZED LUMP CRAB MEAT, PICKED OVER FOR SHELLS

¼ CUP DRY SHERRY

In a 5½-quart Dutch oven, cook the bacon over medium heat until crisp. With a slotted spoon, remove the bacon to a paper towel to drain and set aside.

Add the onions and garlic to the hot bacon fat and cook, stirring frequently, until wilted, about 3 minutes. Add the sweet potato, red peppers, and Scotch Bonnet or jalapeño peppers. Cook for 5 minutes. Stir in the vegetable or chicken stock and 2 tablespoons of the chopped cilantro. Bring to a boil, reduce the heat, and simmer, uncovered, for about 10 minutes.

Stir in the zucchini, corn, tomatoes, cumin, jerk seasoning, chili powder, and salt and pepper to taste. Cook for 5 to 7 minutes. Stir in the milk mixed with cornstarch, Tabasco, and black beans. Bring to a boil and simmer until the soup thickens slightly and the beans are heated through, about 5 minutes.

Stir in the crab meat and cook for 2 minutes, or until the crab is heated through. Remove from the heat, stir in the dry sherry, and top with the remaining 4 tablespoons of chopped cilantro and the chopped bacon just before serving.

NEW ENGLAND CLAM CHOWDER

The term chowder comes from the French word chaudiere, *referring to the caldron that fishermen use to transform their fresh catch into thick fish stew. I like to serve this rich and creamy chowder for Sunday supper. It is comfort food at its best and seems to nourish my body and soul for the busy week ahead. What's even better, it is ready in less than 30 minutes, so no advance planning is needed if I get a sudden craving at the last minute. You can lighten this recipe by substituting 1 tablespoon of olive oil for the bacon, replacing the heavier half and half or cream with milk, and omitting the butter altogether.*

Serves 8

3 (6½ ounce) cans minced clams

2 onions, chopped

1 red pepper, seeded and chopped

6 strips of bacon, coarsely chopped

2 cups fish or chicken stock, preferably homemade

2 baking potatoes, scrubbed and finely diced (do not peel)

1 teaspoon salt

½ teaspoon pepper

Dash of Tabasco

4 cups half and half or heavy cream

1 cup milk mixed with 2 tablespoons cornstarch

4 tablespoons butter, softened

1 (15½ ounce) can creamed corn

3 tablespoons chopped fresh parsley

Drain the clams, reserving the liquid. In a 5½-quart Dutch oven over medium-high heat, cook the onions and the red pepper with the bacon until the bacon is golden brown, about 5 to 8 minutes. Remove about 2 tablespoons of the drippings and discard.

Stir in the reserved clam broth, fish or chicken stock, diced potatoes, salt, pepper, and Tabasco. Cover and simmer until potatoes are tender, about 15 to 20 minutes.

Stir in the half and half or heavy cream, milk-cornstarch mixture, butter, creamed corn, and clams. Cook over medium heat, stirring constantly until thickened, allowing the mixture to come just to a boil. Add salt and pepper to taste. Stir in the chopped parsley just before serving.

Manhattan-Style Clam Chowder is a tomato-based concoction that is spicier than its northern cousin, New England Clam Chowder. With its bold color and lusty flavors, Manhattan-Style Clam Chowder is even more satisfying to me than its creamy counterpart. Try both recipes from this book, then decide which you prefer. Unlike the cream-based version, which tends to separate or curdle upon thawing, this soup will freeze very well for up to two months.

Serves 8

3 (6½ OUNCE) CANS MINCED CLAMS

2 ONIONS, HALVED, PEELED, AND THINLY SLICED

6 STRIPS OF BACON, COARSELY CHOPPED

2 CUPS FISH OR CHICKEN STOCK, PREFERABLY HOMEMADE

3 BAKING POTATOES, PEELED AND FINELY DICED

1 (28 OUNCE) CAN CHOPPED TOMATOES WITH THEIR JUICE

1 (28 OUNCE) CAN CHOPPED TOMATOES WITH ADDED PUREE

2 TABLESPOONS RED WINE VINEGAR

1 TEASPOON SALT

½ TEASPOON BLACK PEPPER

1 TEASPOON SUGAR

½ TEASPOON RED PEPPER FLAKES

1 TABLESPOON CHOPPED FRESH TARRAGON

2 TABLESPOONS CHOPPED FRESH BASIL

4 TO 6 GREEN ONIONS, CHOPPED

Drain the clams, reserving the liquid. In a 5½-quart Dutch oven over medium-high heat, cook the onions with the bacon until the bacon is golden brown, about 5 to 8 minutes.

Stir in the reserved clam broth, fish or chicken stock, potatoes, tomatoes, red wine vinegar, salt, pepper, sugar, and red pepper flakes. Cover and simmer until chowder is thickened and potatoes are tender, about 20 to 25 minutes.

Stir in the reserved clams and the tarragon and basil. Cook over medium heat, stirring occasionally, for 5 minutes. Add additional salt and pepper to taste. Scatter the chowder with the chopped green onions just before serving.

SEAFOOD DUMPLING SOUP WITH GREMOLATA

East meets West in this dazzling seafood soup that combines the flavors of the Orient with those of the sunny Mediterranean. The dumplings are filled with a traditional mix of Asian flavors but get a surprise twist with the addition of pesto and Parmesan cheese. Gremolata is a condiment usually reserved for Italian dishes, but its tart, fresh taste is ideal for this soup.

Serves 8

½ POUND PASTEURIZED LUMP CRAB MEAT, PICKED OVER FOR SHELLS

1 TABLESPOON CHOPPED FRESH GINGER

3 GREEN ONIONS, CHOPPED

2 GARLIC CLOVES, CHOPPED

1 (6½ OUNCE) CAN WATER CHESTNUTS, DRAINED AND CHOPPED

1 TABLESPOON DARK ASIAN SESAME OIL

3 TABLESPOONS COMMERCIAL PESTO

1 CUP FRESHLY GRATED PARMESAN CHEESE

SALT AND FRESHLY GROUND BLACK PEPPER

DASH OF TABASCO

1 POUND (ABOUT 45) POTSTICKER WRAPPERS

10 CUPS CHICKEN STOCK, PREFERABLY HOMEMADE

1 (2 INCH) PIECE OF GINGER, PEELED AND CUT INTO THIN STRIPS

2 CARROTS, SHREDDED

6 GREEN ONIONS, CUT ON THE DIAGONAL INTO ¾-INCH PIECES

1 CUP SNOW PEAS, TIPPED AND TAILED

½ POUND LARGE SHRIMP, PEELED AND DEVEINED

2 TABLESPOONS LIGHT SOY SAUCE

Gremolata

½ CUP GRATED LEMON ZEST

½ CUP CHOPPED FRESH PARSLEY

2 TABLESPOONS CHOPPED FRESH MINT

4 GARLIC CLOVES, FINELY CHOPPED

½ CUP FRESHLY GRATED PARMESAN CHEESE

In a food processor, pulse together the crab meat, chopped ginger, green onions, garlic, water chestnuts, sesame oil, pesto, Parmesan cheese, and salt, pepper, and Tabasco to taste until very finely chopped. Transfer to a medium bowl.

Place 1 heaping teaspoon of the filling slightly off center in a potsticker wrapper. Lightly brush the edges with water. Fold the edges over to form a crescent and firmly press to seal. Repeat with remaining filling and wrappers. You will end up with about 45 filled dumplings.

Bring the stock to a boil in a 5½-quart Dutch oven. Add the strips of ginger, carrots, green onions, and snow peas. Reduce the heat to medium and cook for 1 minute. Stir in the prepared dumplings and shrimp. Cook for 3 to 4 minutes, or just until the shrimp turn pink and curl. Stir in the soy sauce. Ladle into individual bowls and sprinkle with gremolata. Serve at once.

Gremolata

In a medium bowl, combine all ingredients. Store in the refrigerator until ready to use. Tightly covered and refrigerated, gremolata will keep for 2 to 3 days.

Every time I hear the word "succotash" I think of Sylvester the cat. The name actually comes from the Narraganset Indian word msickquatash, which means "boiled whole kernels of corn." Crispy fried hush puppies make a delicious accompaniment to this soup.

Serves 8

¼ CUP BACON DRIPPINGS OR PEANUT OIL

4 CUPS FRESH CORN KERNELS (ABOUT 8 EARS) OR 4 CUPS OF FROZEN CORN

2 ONIONS, CHOPPED

2 RIBS OF CELERY, CHOPPED

1 RED PEPPER, SEEDED AND CHOPPED

1 GREEN PEPPER, SEEDED AND CHOPPED

4 GARLIC CLOVES, CHOPPED

2 BANANA PEPPERS, SEEDED AND FINELY CHOPPED

2 TO 3 TEASPOONS SEAFOOD SEASONING, SUCH AS OLD BAY

1 (16 OUNCE) CAN CRUSHED TOMATOES WITH ADDED PUREE

8 CUPS CHICKEN STOCK, PREFERABLY HOMEMADE

1 (16 OUNCE) PACKAGE FROZEN FORDHOOK LIMA BEANS, DEFROSTED

1 POUND SMALL SHRIMP, PEELED AND DEVEINED

6 GREEN ONIONS, CHOPPED

SALT AND FRESHLY GROUND BLACK PEPPER

TABASCO

In a 5½-quart Dutch oven, heat the bacon drippings or the peanut oil until sizzling. Add the corn, onions, celery, red and green peppers, garlic, and banana peppers. Cook over medium heat, stirring often, until the vegetables are soft, about 15 to 20 minutes.

Add the seafood seasoning, crushed tomatoes, chicken stock, and lima beans. Continue cooking over medium heat for an additional 25 minutes, or until the lima beans are tender.

Stir in the baby shrimp and green onions. Cook for 3 to 4 minutes, or until the shrimp are just cooked and beginning to curl. Add salt and pepper to taste.

Serve piping hot. If desired, sprinkle each serving with Tabasco.

CLASSIC LOBSTER BISQUE

A bisque is a thick, rich soup, usually consisting of pureed seafood or vegetables and cream. This version gets a double shot of flavor from cognac and the lobster shells that are simmered in the soup base. The curry powder adds a subtle taste and a beautiful golden color. I serve this soup on very special occasions.

Serves 4 to 6

4 TABLESPOONS BUTTER

2 TABLESPOONS OLIVE OIL

8 SHALLOTS, FINELY CHOPPED

2 CARROTS, DICED

1 TEASPOON CURRY POWDER

4 FRESH OR FROZEN LOBSTER TAILS (ABOUT 1½ POUNDS)

¼ CUP COGNAC

5 CUPS FISH STOCK, PREFERABLY HOMEMADE

2 CUPS DRY WHITE WINE

¾ CUP LONG-GRAIN RICE

2 TABLESPOONS CHOPPED FRESH TARRAGON

2 CUPS HEAVY CREAM

SALT AND WHITE PEPPER

PINCH OF PAPRIKA

1 TO 2 TABLESPOONS ORANGE JUICE

¼ CUP SNIPPED FRESH CHIVES

In a 5½-quart Dutch oven over medium heat, melt the butter with the olive oil. Add the shallots, carrots, and curry powder. Cook for about 5 minutes, or until shallots are translucent and tender.

Add the lobster tails and cook for 5 minutes. (They will begin to turn a bright orange.) Stir in the cognac, fish stock, and wine. Cook the lobster tails for another 5 minutes. Remove the lobster from the pot. When cool enough to handle, extract the meat and set aside. Add the lobster shells back to the pot, along with the rice and tarragon. Simmer for about 20 minutes, or until the rice is tender.

Remove the lobster shells and discard. Cut the meat from 2 of the lobster tails into chunks. Place the chunks of lobster meat and the soup base in a food processor. Puree until smooth. Strain the puree through a wire strainer and return to the pot.

Add the cream, salt and white pepper to taste, paprika, and orange juice. Gently reheat until just below a boil.

With a sharp knife, thinly slice the remaining 2 lobster tails. Ladle soup into individual bowls. Garnish each with some of the thinly sliced lobster meat and a sprinkling of chives.

The sweetness of parsnips and oysters nicely complements the refined anise taste of tarragon and Pernod in this classic dish. The name of the recipe refers to millionaire John D. Rockefeller, and rightly so. It's an extremely rich dish.

Serves 8

2 (16 OUNCE) CONTAINERS FRESH OYSTERS, UNDRAINED

2 ONIONS, CHOPPED

6 PARSNIPS, PEELED AND THINLY SLICED

1 CUP SLICED MUSHROOMS

8 STRIPS OF BACON, COARSELY CHOPPED

3 CUPS CHICKEN STOCK, PREFERABLY HOMEMADE

1 TEASPOON SALT

½ TEASPOON BLACK PEPPER

1 TEASPOON SUGAR

DASH OF TABASCO

2 (10 OUNCE) PACKAGES FROZEN CHOPPED SPINACH, DEFROSTED AND SQUEEZED DRY

4 CUPS HEAVY CREAM

4 TABLESPOONS BUTTER

1 TABLESPOON LIME JUICE

1 TO 2 TABLESPOONS PERNOD OR OTHER ANISE-FLAVORED LIQUEUR (OPTIONAL)

1 TABLESPOON CHOPPED FRESH TARRAGON

2 TABLESPOONS CHOPPED FRESH PARSLEY

PAPRIKA

Drain the oysters, reserving the liquid. In a 4½-quart Dutch oven over medium-high heat, combine the onions, parsnips, and mushrooms with the bacon. Sauté until the bacon is golden brown, about 10 minutes.

Stir in the drained oyster juice, chicken stock, salt, pepper, sugar, and Tabasco. Simmer, covered, for about 15 to 20 minutes, or until the vegetables are tender.

Add the oysters and chopped spinach. Cook for 3 minutes, or until the oysters just begin to curl around the edges.

Stir in the cream and butter. Cook over medium heat, stirring constantly until thickened. Do not allow the mixture to boil. Taste and adjust the salt and pepper to your liking.

Stir in the lime juice, Pernod, tarragon, and parsley just before serving. Ladle into individual serving bowls and dust with paprika.

DIXIELAND CIOPPINO

Cioppino was invented by Italian immigrants on the fishing wharfs of San Fransisco Bay. This adaptation utilizes some distinct Southern products: Mississippi farm-raised catfish and crayfish from the rice-growing lands of Louisiana and the Carolinas. Serve this soup with crusty garlic French bread and ice-cold beer or a hearty merlot.

Serves 8

¼ cup olive oil

3 onions, halved, peeled, and thinly sliced

3 carrots, shredded

3 ribs of celery, thinly sliced

2 fennel bulbs, halved, tough core removed, and thinly sliced

6 garlic cloves, chopped

1 (28 ounce) can chopped tomatoes with their juice

¼ cup tomato paste

2 cups red wine

1 teaspoon red pepper flakes

1 cup assorted chopped fresh herbs (parsley, basil, thyme leaves, tarragon, and oregano), divided

1 teaspoon fennel seed

Salt and freshly ground black pepper

Grated zest of 2 oranges

4 cups fish stock, preferably homemade

1 pound catfish fillets, cut into 1-inch chunks

1 pound crayfish tails, peeled

1 pound mussels, scrubbed, rinsed well, and debearded

In a 5½-quart Dutch oven with a tight-fitting lid, heat the olive oil. Add the onions, carrots, celery, fennel, and garlic. Cook over medium-high heat until the vegetables are soft, about 10 minutes. Add the chopped tomatoes, tomato paste, red wine, red pepper flakes, ½ cup of the chopped herbs, fennel seed, and salt and pepper to taste. Bring to a boil, cover, and reduce the heat to a simmer. Cook for 1 hour, stirring occasionally.

Stir in the orange zest, fish stock, catfish, crayfish tails, and mussels. Cover and cook for 10 minutes, or until the fish is white and opaque, the crayfish tails are coral, and the mussels have opened. Discard any mussels that do not open.

Stir in the remaining ½ cup of herbs and adjust the seasonings with additional salt and pepper if needed. Ladle into shallow soup bowls and serve at once.

FRESH & SALTED CODFISH CHOWDER

Salt cod is cod that has been salted and dried. It develops an intense flavor that is richer than its rather bland-tasting fresh counterpart. Salt cod must be reconstituted before use; the soaking process also removes excess salt.

Serves 8

1 POUND SALTED COD, SOAKED IN WATER OVERNIGHT, RINSED, AND DRAINED

2 CUPS MILK

2 CUPS WATER

1 BAY LEAF

2 SPRIGS OF THYME

4 SPRIGS OF PARSLEY

1 POUND FRESH BONELESS COD FILLETS

4 TABLESPOONS BUTTER

3 RIBS OF CELERY, CHOPPED

2 ONIONS, CHOPPED

2 SWEET POTATOES, PEELED AND CUT INTO ½-INCH DICE

1 (16 OUNCE) PACKAGE FROZEN BABY LIMA BEANS, DEFROSTED

3 CUPS FISH STOCK, PREFERABLY HOMEMADE

3 CUPS MILK

6 GREEN ONIONS, CHOPPED

⅓ CUP SNIPPED FRESH CHIVES

¼ CUP CHOPPED FRESH PARSLEY

1 TEASPOON Tabasco

1 TEASPOON DRY MUSTARD

2 TABLESPOONS Worcestershire SAUCE

SALT AND FRESHLY GROUND BLACK PEPPER

OYSTER CRACKERS

In a 3½-quart Dutch oven, mix together the soaked and drained salted cod, milk, water, bay leaf, thyme sprigs, and parsley sprigs. Bring to a boil, reduce the heat to low, and cook for 15 minutes. Add the fresh cod and cook for 8 to 10 minutes. Drain and remove the fish to a large bowl to cool, discarding the flavoring ingredients. Flake the fish with a fork and set aside.

Meanwhile, in a 5½-quart Dutch oven, melt the butter over medium heat until sizzling. Add the celery and onions and cook until the onions are translucent, about 5 minutes. Add the sweet potatoes, lima beans, and fish stock. Bring to a boil, reduce the heat, and simmer, covered, for 25 minutes, or until the beans and potatoes are tender.

Remove the cover and stir in the flaked fish, milk, green onions, chives, parsley, Tabasco, dry mustard, Worcestershire sauce, and salt and pepper to taste. Bring to a boil and simmer for 5 minutes. Serve steaming hot, topped with oyster crackers.

SMOKED TROUT CHOWDER

The savory flavor of smoked trout brings this otherwise common chowder to life. I prefer the beautiful pink flesh of smoked trout, but any other smoked white fish would work well in this recipe. Be sure to pick through and discard all the tiny pin bones before adding the fish to the soup.

Serves 8

4 STRIPS OF BACON, COARSELY CHOPPED

2 ONIONS, CHOPPED

1 RED PEPPER, SEEDED AND CHOPPED

3 RIBS OF CELERY, CHOPPED

2 BAKING POTATOES, PEELED AND CUT INTO ½-INCH DICE

8 CUPS CHICKEN STOCK, PREFERABLY HOMEMADE

1 (10 OUNCE) PACKAGE FROZEN BABY LIMA BEANS, DEFROSTED

1 (15½ OUNCE) CAN CREAMED CORN

SALT AND FRESHLY GROUND BLACK PEPPER

I TABLESPOON CORNSTARCH

1½ CUPS HALF AND HALF OR MILK

1 TABLESPOON WORCESTERSHIRE SAUCE

2 SMOKED TROUT, SKINNED, BONED, AND FLAKED
   INTO 1-INCH PIECES

3 TABLESPOONS CHOPPED FRESH PARSLEY

2 TABLESPOONS CHOPPED FRESH DILL

OYSTER CRACKERS

In a 4½-quart Dutch oven over medium-high heat, combine the bacon, onions, red pepper, and celery. Cook, stirring occasionally, until the bacon is crisp and the vegetables are tender, about 5 to 8 minutes.

Add the potatoes, chicken stock, and lima beans. Bring to a boil, reduce the heat, and simmer, uncovered, for 15 minutes. Stir in the corn and salt and pepper to taste and cook for 5 minutes.

In a 2-cup measuring cup, whisk together the cornstarch, half and half or milk, and Worcestershire sauce until smooth. Stir into the simmering soup, along with the smoked trout. Bring just to a boil, stir in the parsley and dill, and ladle into serving bowls. Serve hot, passing the oyster crackers separately.

PENNE PASTA & SMOKED SALMON SOUP WITH TOMATOES, PEPPERED VODKA & CREAM

Quite simply, this soup is fabulous. Add a tossed salad with sliced beets, a brioche roll, and a bottle of white wine, and you're on your way to a memorable evening. It's easy to make your own pepper-flavored vodka. In a clean glass bottle, mix together 2 cups of vodka, 6 dried hot peppers, 1 tablespoon black peppercorns, and 1 teaspoon red pepper flakes. Steep for about one week in a cool, dark place, then strain and pour into a clean bottle with a tight-fitting lid. This flavored vodka will last indefinitely.

Serves 8

¼ CUP OLIVE OIL

1 RED ONION, HALVED, PEELED, AND THINLY SLICED

2 RED PEPPERS, SEEDED AND THINLY SLICED

1 GREEN PEPPER, SEEDED AND THINLY SLICED

4 GARLIC CLOVES, CHOPPED

½ TEASPOON RED PEPPER FLAKES

SALT AND FRESHLY GROUND BLACK PEPPER

1 (28 OUNCE) CAN CHOPPED PLUM TOMATOES WITH THEIR JUICE

1 TEASPOON SUGAR

8 CUPS CHICKEN STOCK, PREFERABLY HOMEMADE

12 OUNCES UNCOOKED PENNE PASTA

¼ CUP PEPPER-FLAVORED VODKA

1 CUP HEAVY CREAM

8 OUNCES THINLY SLICED SMOKED SALMON

¼ CUP CHOPPED FRESH PARSLEY

1 CUP FRESHLY GRATED PARMESAN CHEESE, PLUS ADDITIONAL FOR GARNISH

ADDITIONAL PARSLEY

In an 5½-quart Dutch oven, heat the oil over medium-high heat. Add the red onion, red peppers, green pepper, garlic, red pepper flakes, and salt and pepper to taste. Cook over medium heat for about 3 to 4 minutes, stirring often to prevent the garlic from burning.

Add the chopped tomatoes and sugar and simmer, uncovered, for about 15 minutes, or until the sauce begins to thicken.

Add the chicken stock and pasta. Bring to a boil and cook for 8 to 10 minutes, or until the pasta is tender but not mushy.

Add the vodka and stir to mix. Add the cream, smoked salmon, parsley, and Parmesan cheese. Heat to just below a boil.

Sprinkle with additional Parmesan cheese and parsley and serve at once.

MOSTLY VEGETABLE SOUPS

Roasted Red Pepper and Corn Chowder

Burgundy Four-Onion Soup with Fennel

Baked Acorn Squash and Gruyère Soup

Ribollita

Boston Baked Bean Soup with
Steamed Molasses Brown Bread

Gingered Sweet Potato and Apple Soup

Roasted Garlic Soup with Green Grapes

Cheesy Macaroni Soup

Winter Vegetable Bourguignonne Soup

Curried Pumpkin Soup with Citrus Yogurt Cheese

Yukon Gold Potato and Celery Root Soup with
Crispy Flatbread

Yellow Winter Vegetable Soup

White Winter Vegetable Soup

Butternut Squash and Apple Soup

Roasted Red Pepper and Basil Soup

African Peanut Soup with Harissa Sauce

Exotic Dried Mushroom and Barley Soup

Hot Curried Cream of Tomato Soup

White Cheddar and Vegetable Soup

Best Borscht

Warm and Soothing Chunky Caribbean Gazpacho

Roasted Pepita (Pumpkin Seed) and Tomato-Rice Soup

Pureed Lentil Soup

Asparagus and Dill Soup

Tex-Mex Black Bean Soup

Saffron Couscous Soup with Vegetables and Dried Cherries

Corn, Black Bean, Serrano Chile, and Jicama Soup

Stilton Cheese and Scallion Soup

Simple Onion Soup with Roquefort and Chive Toasts

Splendid Split Pea Soup

Brie and Broccoli Soup

Pan-Roasted Barley Soup

Speedy "Cream" of Broccoli Soup

Hoppin' John Soup with Turnip Greens

Szechwan Asparagus Noodle Soup

Collard Green, Pinto, and Sweet Potato Soup with
Cheddar Corn Mini-Muffins

Roasted Chestnut and Apple Soup

ROASTED RED PEPPER & CORN CHOWDER

For this recipe, the fresher the corn the better. Once corn is picked, its sugars begin a gradual conversion to starch, which lessens the corn's natural sweetness. I prefer Silver Queen, a white corn with small, compact kernels. If you use yellow (or frozen) corn, add 1 teaspoon of sugar to brighten the flavor.

Serves 8 to 10

4 RED PEPPERS

8 STRIPS OF BACON, DICED

2 ONIONS, CHOPPED

4 GREEN ONIONS, CHOPPED

2 RIBS OF CELERY, THINLY SLICED

2 CARROTS, SHREDDED

4 GARLIC CLOVES, CHOPPED

1 CUP SLICED MUSHROOMS

⅓ CUP FLOUR

1 TEASPOON SALT

FRESHLY GROUND BLACK PEPPER

½ TEASPOON RED PEPPER FLAKES

2 TEASPOONS POULTRY SEASONING

4 CUPS FRESH WHITE CORN KERNELS (ABOUT 8 EARS)

8 CUPS CHICKEN STOCK, PREFERABLY HOMEMADE

2 CUPS CREAM OR HALF AND HALF

2 TABLESPOONS FRESH THYME LEAVES

Preheat the broiler. Cut the red peppers in half lengthwise and remove the seeds and membranes. Place the peppers, skin side up, on a foil-lined baking sheet. Place in the oven, about 6 inches from the heat source. Broil until the peppers are charred and blackened, about 10 minutes. Remove from the oven and carefully place the hot peppers in a gallon-sized zip-top freezer bag. Seal the bag and set aside. When peppers are cool enough to handle, slip the blackened skins off and discard. Cut peppers into thin strips. Set aside.

In a heavy 5½-quart Dutch oven, fry the bacon until crisp, remove with a slotted spoon, and drain on paper towels, reserving the drippings.

Add to the drippings the onions, green onions, celery, carrots, and garlic. Cook over medium-high heat for about 5 minutes. Lower the heat to medium, add the mushrooms, and cook for 5 minutes. Add the flour, salt, pepper to taste, red pepper flakes, and poultry seasoning. Cook, stirring constantly, for 2 minutes.

Add the corn and chicken stock. Bring to a boil, reduce the heat, and simmer, covered, for 10 minutes. Remove the lid, stir in the cream or half and half and the roasted red pepper strips, and cook until just heated through. Do not let the cream boil. Stir in the thyme leaves and the reserved chopped bacon. Serve at once.

BURGUNDY FOUR-ONION SOUP WITH FENNEL

The secret to this French bistro-style soup is to caramelize the onions at the beginning of the recipe. In order for the caramelized flavor to develop, the mixture must become a rich pecan brown. I like to use chicken stock in this soup instead of the expected beef stock. Combining beef stock and Burgundy wine in the same soup make for too many strong flavors, in my opinion. Do not use any wine labeled "cooking wine." Sodium is usually the second ingredient on a cooking wine's label. Remember the rule: If you cannot drink it, don't cook with it!

Serves 8

6 LEEKS, CLEANED, TRIMMED, AND THINLY SLICED

2 YELLOW ONIONS, HALVED, PEELED, AND THINLY SLICED

2 RED ONIONS, HALVED, PEELED, AND THINLY SLICED

6 SHALLOTS, CHOPPED

1 TO 2 FENNEL BULBS, HALVED, TOUGH CORE REMOVED, AND THINLY SLICED (RESERVE THE FRONDS)

¼ CUP OLIVE OIL

½ TEASPOON SALT

½ TEASPOON BLACK PEPPER

¼ CUP FLOUR

6 CUPS CHICKEN STOCK, PREFERABLY HOMEMADE

2 CUPS BURGUNDY WINE

1 TABLESPOON CHOPPED FRESH ROSEMARY

¼ TEASPOON FRESHLY GRATED NUTMEG

Gruyère Croûtes

8 SLICES FRENCH BREAD

2 TABLESPOONS OLIVE OIL

½ CUP GRATED GRUYÈRE CHEESE

In a 5½-quart Dutch oven, combine the leeks, yellow onions, red onions, shallots, and fennel slices with the olive oil. Sprinkle this mixture with the salt and pepper. Cook over medium-high heat until the onions begin to caramelize, about 30 to 40 minutes. You will need to stir occasionally to prevent sticking.

Stir in the flour and cook for 2 to 3 minutes longer. Slowly whisk in the chicken stock and red wine. Bring the mixture to a boil, reduce the heat, and simmer for 20 minutes.

Just before serving the soup, stir in the rosemary and nutmeg. Taste for seasoning and add salt and pepper as needed.

Ladle the hot soup into individual soup bowls and top each with a Gruyère Croûte. Chop the reserved fennel fronds and sprinkle over the soup and bread. Serve at once.

Gruyère Croûtes

Preheat the oven to 400°F. Place bread on a baking sheet and brush each piece with some of the olive oil. Bake for about 5 minutes, or until golden. Remove the bread from the oven and divide the cheese among the 8 slices. Return to the oven and bake until the cheese melts and just begins to bubble, about 2 minutes.

BAKED ACORN SQUASH & GRUYÈRE SOUP

Served in squash shells, this soup is a beautiful addition to a holiday table. I like to split the squash in half lengthwise so that it retains the silhouette of an acorn. If the shell will not sit up straight, slice a thin portion off the bottom, being careful not to cut into the bowl of the squash.

Serves 8

4 (1 POUND EACH) ACORN SQUASH, BLEMISH-FREE

4 TABLESPOONS BUTTER

1 TABLESPOON CHOPPED FRESH ROSEMARY

1 ONION, CHOPPED

2 GARLIC CLOVES, CHOPPED

3 CARROTS, CHOPPED

1 SWEET POTATO, PEELED AND CUT INTO ½-INCH DICE

6 CUPS CHICKEN STOCK, PREFERABLY HOMEMADE

1 TEASPOON SALT

½ TEASPOON WHITE PEPPER

2 CUPS HALF AND HALF

4 (1 INCH THICK) SLICES ITALIAN-STYLE BREAD, TORN INTO PIECES

2 CUPS GRATED GRUYÈRE CHEESE

FRESHLY GRATED NUTMEG

Cut the acorn squash in half lengthwise. Remove and discard the seeds and fibers. With a melon baller or grapefruit knife, carefully remove the pulp, leaving a ½-inch rim around the squash. Chop the pulp and set the hollowed-out squash halves aside.

In a 4½-quart Dutch oven, melt the butter over medium heat and stir in the rosemary. Cook for 1 minute, or until very fragrant. Add the chopped squash, onion, garlic, carrots, and sweet potato. Cook over medium heat for 15 minutes, or until softened.

Stir in the chicken stock and salt and white pepper. Bring to a boil. Reduce the heat and simmer, covered, for 20 minutes. Strain the solids in a colander and transfer them to a food processor. Return the liquid to the pot. Puree the squash mixture until very smooth and creamy. Transfer the pureed squash back into the pot. Stir in the half and half and bring just to a boil. Taste and add salt and pepper if necessary.

Preheat the oven to 400°F. Place the squash halves on a baking sheet. Layer the torn bread and cheese in each individual squash half. Carefully pour the soup into the squash. Bake for 10 to 12 minutes, or until soup is thick and bubbly and the cheese has melted. Serve at once.

RIBOLLITA

Ribollita is the Italian word meaning "twice boiled." This term refers to the addition of bread toward the end of this thick and lusty soup's cooking time. For an interesting change, replace the navy beans with one of the 5-, 7-, or 13-bean prepackaged varieties sold in most supermarkets today.

Serves 8 to 10

8 STRIPS BACON, CHOPPED

2 ONIONS, HALVED, PEELED, AND THINLY SLICED

8 GARLIC CLOVES, THINLY SLICED

1 POUND BABY CARROTS, SCRAPED

4 RIBS OF CELERY, THINLY SLICED

4 GREEN ONIONS, CHOPPED

12 CUPS CHICKEN STOCK, PREFERABLY HOMEMADE

2 TABLESPOONS CHOPPED FRESH ROSEMARY

1 BAY LEAF, CRUMBLED

1 POUND DRIED NAVY BEANS, PRESOAKED (SEE PAGE 9)

1 TEASPOON SALT

½ TEASPOON BLACK PEPPER

1 TEASPOON RED PEPPER FLAKES

½ SMALL HEAD RED CABBAGE, THINLY SLICED (ABOUT 4 CUPS)

8 (1 INCH THICK) SLICES ITALIAN-STYLE BREAD,
   TORN INTO PIECES

2 TABLESPOONS CHOPPED FRESH BASIL

2 CUPS FRESHLY GRATED PARMESAN OR ROMANO CHEESE

EXTRA-VIRGIN OLIVE OIL

In a 5½-quart Dutch oven over medium-high heat, cook the bacon until some of the fat is rendered, about 2 minutes. Add the onions, garlic, baby carrots, celery, and green onions. Cook until the vegetables are just beginning to brown, about 15 minutes.

Add the chicken stock, rosemary, and bay leaf. Bring to a boil. Add the beans, salt, pepper, and red pepper flakes. Cover and simmer for 45 minutes. Stir in the red cabbage and cook until the navy beans are tender, about 30 minutes.

Stir in the bread and simmer until the bread begins to fall apart and the soup thickens, about 10 minutes.

Stir in the basil and adjust seasonings with additional salt and pepper if necessary. Top the soup with grated cheese and ladle into individual serving bowls. Drizzle each serving with extra-virgin olive oil. Serve at once.

BOSTON BAKED BEAN SOUP

I like to serve this soup during that magical season when the leaves are changing. The wonderful aromas that fill the kitchen while this hearty soup is baking, coupled with the burnished red and gold colors outside, alert my senses that my favorite time of year has arrived.

Serves 8

10 strips of bacon, cut into 1-inch pieces

2 onions, peeled, halved, and thinly sliced

6 garlic cloves, chopped

3 cups dried navy or white beans, presoaked (see page 9)

⅔ cup brown sugar

⅔ cup dark molasses

½ cup Dijon mustard

2 tablespoons dry mustard

1 teaspoon ground ginger

1½ cups chili sauce or ketchup

1 (16 ounce) can chopped tomatoes with their juice

Salt and freshly ground black pepper

12 cups beef stock or water

Preheat the oven to 300°F. In a 5½-quart Dutch oven with a tight-fitting lid, combine the bacon, onions, and garlic. Cook over medium heat until the bacon is lightly browned and the onions are wilted. Add the drained beans, brown sugar, molasses, Dijon mustard, dry mustard, ginger, chili sauce or ketchup, tomatoes, and salt and pepper to taste, and mix well. Add the beef stock or water. Bring to a boil. Cover the pot and place in the oven. Cook for 6 hours, stirring every 2 hours or so. Remove the lid and continue baking for 1 to 2 hours longer, or until the beans are tender and the color of deep caramel and the soup is thick and bubbly.

Ladle into bowls and serve with Steamed Molasses Brown Bread.

STEAMED MOLASSES BROWN BREAD

This slightly sweet, very dense, moist steamed bread makes a wonderful accompaniment to Boston Baked Bean Soup. Any leftover bread is perfect for breakfast thinly sliced and toasted, with cream cheese and fruit preserves or drizzled with maple syrup.

Makes 1 loaf

¼ CUP CORNMEAL (NOT CORNMEAL MIX)

½ CUP RYE FLOUR

¼ CUP ALL-PURPOSE FLOUR

½ CUP WHOLE-WHEAT FLOUR

1 TEASPOON BAKING SODA

½ TEASPOON BAKING POWDER

½ TEASPOON SALT

½ CUP DARK MOLASSES

1 CUP BUTTERMILK

½ CUP RAISINS, LIGHTLY DUSTED WITH 1 TABLESPOON
  ALL-PURPOSE FLOUR

Grease and flour a clean (1 pound) coffee container, line the bottom with a disc of waxed paper, and grease and flour the paper. Set aside.

In a large bowl, sift together the dry ingredients. In a smaller bowl, whisk together the dark molasses and buttermilk. Slowly pour the liquid ingredients into the bowl containing the flours. Stir just enough to blend. Do not overmix. Fold in the raisins and pour the batter into the prepared can. Double a piece of aluminum foil, lightly butter one side, and place the foil, buttered side down, over the can. Tie the foil securely in place with kitchen twine.

Place a cake rack in an 8-quart stockpot with a lid. Place the can on the rack and fill the pot with enough hot water to come halfway up the sides of the can. Cover the pot with the lid. Bring the water to a boil, reduce the heat, and simmer for 1½ to 2 hours, or until a wooden skewer inserted into the bread comes out clean and the bread springs back when lightly pressed. (It may be necessary to add more hot water during the steaming time. You want to maintain a level of water halfway up the side of the can.)

Remove the can and rack from the pot and allow the bread to cool on the rack for a few minutes, then carefully remove the bread and allow it to cool on its side. For uniform pieces, slice the bread with a serrated knife.

GINGERED SWEET POTATO & APPLE SOUP

Whenever I make this soup ahead, I add the cream at the last minute, just after reheating the soup. Baking the sweet potatoes in the oven allows their natural sugars to concentrate in the pulp. Sweet, crisp Golden Delicious or crunchy, tart Granny Smith apples make excellent substitutes if you can't find Stayman Winesaps.

Serves 8

5 SWEET POTATOES, SCRUBBED

2 TABLESPOONS CANDIED GINGER, FINELY CHOPPED

3 TO 4 LEEKS, CLEANED, TRIMMED, AND THINLY SLICED

6 TO 8 GREEN ONIONS, THINLY SLICED

3 STAYMAN WINESAP APPLES, PEELED, CORED, AND SLICED

4 CUPS CHICKEN STOCK, PREFERABLY HOMEMADE

GRATED ZEST OF 1 LEMON

SALT AND FRESHLY GROUND BLACK PEPPER

3 CUPS APPLE CIDER

¼ TEASPOON GROUND CINNAMON

FRESHLY GRATED NUTMEG

1 CUP HEAVY CREAM, LIGHTLY WHIPPED TO A MOUSSE-LIKE
   CONSISTENCY

2 TABLESPOONS SNIPPED FRESH CHIVES

½ CUP SHREDDED PARMESAN CHEESE

½ CUP CHOPPED PECANS OR WALNUTS, LIGHTLY
   TOASTED (SEE PAGE 13)

Preheat the oven to 400°F. Pierce each sweet potato several times with a fork and place in the oven directly on the rack. Bake until soft, about 1 hour.

Meanwhile, in a 4½-quart Dutch oven, combine the candied ginger, leeks, green onions, apple slices, chicken stock, lemon zest, and salt and pepper to taste. Bring to a boil, reduce the heat, and simmer, uncovered, for 15 to 20 minutes, or until the leeks are very tender.

Split the sweet potatoes in half and scoop out the pulp, discarding the skins. Add the sweet potato to the hot stock and simmer for 5 minutes.

Place this mixture, in batches if needed, into a food processor or blender and puree until smooth. Return the pureed mixture to the pot and stir in the apple cider. Bring to just below a boil. Add the cinnamon and nutmeg. Adjust to taste with additional salt and pepper. Whisk in the whipped cream.

Ladle into a beautiful soup tureen or individual bowls. Top with chives, Parmesan cheese, and toasted nuts. Serve at once.

ROASTED GARLIC SOUP WITH GREEN GRAPES

Don't let the number of garlic cloves in this delicious soup alarm you. When garlic is roasted, it develops a mellow, almost nut-like taste. The sweet green grapes offer an interesting taste and textural contrast. This marriage of soup and bread is sometimes called a panade, although traditionally a panade utilizes bread crumbs.

Serves 8

5 HEADS GARLIC, SEPARATED INTO CLOVES AND PEELED (ABOUT 60 CLOVES)

2 ONIONS, HALVED, PEELED, AND THINLY SLICED

¼ CUP OLIVE OIL

4 TABLESPOONS BUTTER, MELTED

½ TEASPOON SALT

½ TEASPOON BLACK PEPPER

1 TABLESPOON FLOUR

8 CUPS CHICKEN STOCK, PREFERABLY HOMEMADE

8 SLICES FRENCH BREAD, TORN INTO PIECES

½ CUP GRATED GRUYÈRE CHEESE

1 CUP SEEDLESS GREEN GRAPES, CUT IN HALF

Preheat the oven to 400°F. In a large, oven-proof baking dish, toss the garlic and onions with the olive oil and melted butter. Sprinkle this mixture with salt, pepper, and flour.

Cover the baking dish with heavy-duty aluminum foil. Place in the oven and roast for 1 to 1½ hours, or until garlic is soft.

In a 4½-quart Dutch oven, bring the chicken stock to a boil. Transfer the roasted garlic, onions, and oil and butter to a food processor and puree until smooth. Add this mixture to the stock and blend thoroughly. Taste for seasonings and add salt and pepper as needed.

Divide the French bread among 8 serving bowls. Ladle the soup over the bread and let sit for 1 minute to allow the bread to absorb some the flavors of the soup. Sprinkle each bowl with grated Gruyère cheese and green grapes. Serve at once.

CHEESY MACARONI SOUP

This soup is ready from stovetop to table in less than 20 minutes. Cook the macaroni while making the soup base, mix together, give it a quick run in the oven, and enjoy. Kids of all ages will sing your praises. If desired, mix in 2 cups of cooked, diced chicken or ham before baking.

Serves 8

6 TABLESPOONS BUTTER

⅓ CUP FLOUR

½ TEASPOON SALT

½ TEASPOON BLACK PEPPER

4 CUPS CHICKEN STOCK, PREFERABLY HOMEMADE

4 CUPS MILK

4 CUPS GRATED SWISS AND CHEDDAR CHEESE, MIXED
  (ABOUT 1 POUND), DIVIDED

12 OUNCES COOKED ELBOW MACARONI

1 CUP SEASONED BREAD CRUMBS

In a 4½-quart Dutch oven over medium heat, melt the butter and add the flour, salt, and pepper. Cook over low heat, stirring all the time, until the mixture is smooth and bubbly, about 2 minutes.

Add the chicken stock and milk, bring to a boil, and cook for 2 minutes. Remove from the heat and add 3 cups of the cheese, stirring until the mixture is melted and smooth. Stir in the cooked macaroni.

Preheat the oven to 350°F. Divide the soup among 8 ovenproof serving bowls. Top each serving with the remaining 1 cup of grated cheese and the bread crumbs. Place bowls on a baking sheet and bake for 10 minutes, or until soup is bubbly and the top is golden brown. Serve at once.

WINTER VEGETABLE BOURGUIGNONNE SOUP

By stirring in the chopped herbs just before serving, this hearty soup takes on a surprisingly fresh taste.

Serves 8

2 OUNCES DRIED MUSHROOMS

2 CUPS BURGUNDY WINE

¼ CUP VEGETABLE OIL

2 ONIONS, PEELED, HALVED, AND THINLY SLICED

8 SHALLOTS, QUARTERED

16 GARLIC CLOVES, THINLY SLICED

3 TABLESPOONS FLOUR

2 TABLESPOONS CHOPPED FRESH ROSEMARY

2 SWEET POTATOES, PEELED AND CUT INTO 1-INCH CHUNKS

12 NEW POTATOES, SCRUBBED AND QUARTERED

2 CARROTS, CUT INTO ½-INCH CHUNKS

2 PARSNIPS, PEELED AND CUT INTO ½-INCH CHUNKS

2 TURNIPS, PEELED AND CUT INTO ½-INCH CHUNKS

1 RUTABAGA, PEELED AND CUT INTO ½-INCH CHUNKS

2 BAY LEAVES, CRUMBLED

1 (28 OUNCE) CAN WHOLE TOMATOES WITH THEIR JUICE,
   COARSELY CHOPPED

8 CUPS VEGETABLE STOCK, PREFERABLY HOMEMADE

2 TABLESPOONS CHOPPED FRESH BASIL

2 TABLESPOONS CHOPPED FRESH OREGANO

SALT AND FRESHLY GROUND BLACK PEPPER

½ CUP CHOPPED FRESH PARSLEY

In a medium bowl, combine the dried mushrooms and the red wine. Let sit for 1 hour. With a slotted spoon, remove the mushrooms and strain the wine through a triple thickness of cheesecloth. Coarsely chop the mushrooms and set aside. Reserve the strained wine.

Meanwhile, in a large 5½-quart Dutch oven, heat the oil until sizzling. Stir in the onions, shallots, and garlic. Cook over medium heat, stirring occasionally, until the mixture is a deep mahogany brown, about 30 minutes. Stir in the flour and rosemary. Cook for 5 minutes. Set aside.

Add the sweet potatoes, new potatoes, carrots, parsnips, turnips, and rutabaga. Cook over medium heat, stirring occasionally, until the vegetables begin to crisp on the outside, about 15 minutes.

Stir in the bay leaves, tomatoes, vegetable stock, reserved red wine, and reconstituted mushrooms. Simmer, uncovered, for 45 minutes, or until the vegetables are tender.

Stir in the basil and oregano. Season to taste with salt and pepper. Transfer to individual serving bowls or a soup tureen. Sprinkle with chopped parsley. Serve at once.

CURRIED PUMPKIN SOUP WITH CITRUS YOGURT CHEESE

Canned pumpkin makes this a snap to make. Curry powders differ in India by region, much the same way barbecue sauces do in the United States. Check the ingredient lists of different curry blends. Most will contain the more common dried chiles, red and black pepper, coriander, cardamom, cumin, cinnamon, cloves, mace, nutmeg, and fennel, as well as the more unusual fenugreek, turmeric, tamarind, and saffron. Find a blend that suits your taste.

Serves 8

3 tablespoons butter

4 to 6 leeks, cleaned, trimmed, and thinly sliced

2 to 3 teaspoons curry powder, preferably Madras

6 cups chicken stock, preferably homemade

2 (16 ounce) cans solid packed pumpkin (not pumpkin pie filling)

Grated zest of 1 orange

Salt and freshly ground black pepper

Freshly grated nutmeg

1 cup heavy cream

1 cup yogurt cheese*

2 tablespoons lime juice

2 tablespoons orange juice

1 teaspoon ground ginger

Julienned zest of 2 limes

In a 4½-quart Dutch oven, melt the butter and add the leeks. Cook over medium heat until the leeks soften, about 5 minutes. Do not allow the leeks to brown. Stir in the curry powder and cook for 2 minutes.

Add the chicken stock, pumpkin, orange zest, and salt, pepper, and nutmeg to taste. Bring to a boil, reduce the heat, and simmer, uncovered, for 10 minutes.

Stir in the cream and bring to just below a boil. Adjust seasonings to taste with additional salt and pepper.

In a small bowl, mix together the yogurt cheese, lime juice, orange juice, and ground ginger.

Transfer the soup to a tureen or individual bowls. Top each serving with a dollop of the citrus-yogurt cheese and garnish with lime zest. Serve at once.

*To make yogurt cheese, place 16 ounces of plain nonfat yogurt into a strainer lined with cheesecloth. Suspend over a bowl and refrigerate overnight. Discard the whey (liquid). Makes about 1 cup.

This recipe, together with the flatbread recipe that follows, was adapted from a recipe in Gourmet *magazine. Although any all-purpose potato will suffice, Yukon Gold potatoes offer a beautiful golden color and rich, buttery taste. If celery root (sometimes called celeriac) is unavailable, chop enough celery hearts (1 small bunch) to yield 3 cups. While you are making the bread, keep the soup covered at room temperature. The flavors will mingle into a sublime taste sensation. Gently reheat the soup before serving.*

Serves 8

4 POUNDS YUKON GOLD POTATOES, PEELED AND CUT INTO 1-INCH CUBES

1½ POUNDS CELERY ROOT, PEELED AND CUT INTO ½-INCH CUBES

3 LEEKS, CLEANED, TRIMMED, AND THINLY SLICED

8 CUPS CHICKEN STOCK, PREFERABLY HOMEMADE

SALT AND FRESHLY GROUND BLACK PEPPER

FRESH HERB BOUQUET MADE WITH 6 SPRIGS OF PARSLEY, 1 LEMON WEDGE, AND 1 BAY LEAF, TIED IN CHEESECLOTH

½ TEASPOON GROUND GINGER

½ CUP SNIPPED FRESH CHIVES

FRESHLY GRATED NUTMEG

In a heavy 5½-quart Dutch oven, combine the potatoes, celery root, leeks, chicken stock, salt and pepper to taste, herb bouquet, and ground ginger. Bring to a boil, reduce the heat, and simmer, partially covered, for 1 hour, or until the vegetables are tender. Discard the herb bouquet. Strain through a colander, returning the broth to the Dutch oven. With a slotted spoon, remove 1 cup of the solids for the flatbread and set aside.*

In a food processor or blender, puree the remaining solids until smooth and creamy. Return to the pot and stir to combine. Adjust seasonings with additional salt and pepper if necessary. When ready to serve, stir in the snipped chives. Ladle into individual bowls and top each serving with a fresh grating of nutmeg. Serve with Crispy Flatbread.

*If you do not plan to make the flatbread, puree all the solids and use in the soup.

CRISPY FLATBREAD

You can vary this recipe by adding ½ to ¾ cup of any one of the following to the risen batter: chopped sun-dried tomatoes, chopped green onions, chopped Greek black olives, chopped roasted red pepper, crumbled or shredded cheese, sunflower seeds, or chopped nuts. The possibilities are endless!

Makes one 13 x 9-inch flatbread

½ CUP MILK, HEATED TO 115°F

1 PACKAGE ACTIVE DRY YEAST

1 TEASPOON SUGAR

1 CUP RESERVED SOLIDS FROM YUKON GOLD POTATO AND
    CELERY ROOT SOUP, COOLED

1 EGG, LIGHTLY BEATEN

3 TABLESPOONS BUTTER, SOFTENED

1½ CUPS BREAD FLOUR

3 TABLESPOONS CHOPPED FRESH ROSEMARY

OLIVE OIL

COARSE KOSHER SALT

In a measuring cup, whisk together the milk, yeast, and sugar. Proof the yeast for 10 minutes, or until very foamy and bubbly. In a large bowl, beat the yeast mixture into the cooled solids, along with the egg and softened butter. Gradually beat in the flour and the rosemary until smooth. The mixture will be more like a batter than a dough. Cover with plastic wrap and let stand at room temperature until the dough doubles in volume, about 1 hour.

Stir the risen batter down with a wooden spoon. Preheat the oven to 375°F. Lightly oil or spray a 13 x 9-inch baking sheet. Using oiled hands, spread the dough thinly and evenly over the baking sheet. Make small indentations with your fingers along the surface of the bread. Drizzle with a little olive oil and coarse salt. Bake for 25 minutes, or until golden. Cut or tear into pieces and serve with Yukon Gold Potato and Celery Root Soup.

I often serve the following two vegetable soups together. The interesting contrast of flavors and colors is highlighted by ladling half of each soup, side by side, into individual serving bowls and garnishing with green onions and paprika. I prefer these soups thick and chunky, but for a smoother consistency, process the solids in a food processor instead of using a potato masher.

Serves 8 to 10

3 CARROTS, COARSELY CHOPPED

2 SWEET POTATOES, PEELED AND COARSELY CHOPPED

1 RUTABAGA, PEELED AND COARSELY CHOPPED

2 GRANNY SMITH APPLES, PEELED, CORED, AND COARSELY
   CHOPPED

10 CUPS CHICKEN STOCK, PREFERABLY HOMEMADE

1 TEASPOON SALT

½ TEASPOON BLACK PEPPER

8 TABLESPOONS (ONE STICK) BUTTER, SOFTENED

¼ TEASPOON FRESHLY GRATED NUTMEG

1 TABLESPOON CHOPPED FRESH ROSEMARY

6 GREEN ONIONS, CHOPPED

1 TEASPOON PAPRIKA

Place the carrots, sweet potatoes, rutabaga, and apples in a 5½-quart Dutch oven and cover with chicken stock. Stir in the salt and pepper. Place over medium-high heat and bring to a boil. Cook until vegetables are very tender, about 25 minutes.

Drain and reserve the stock. Return the cooked vegetables to the pot. Add the butter, nutmeg, and rosemary. Roughly mash vegetables with a potato masher until chunky. Return the stock to the pot and bring to a low simmer. Season with additional salt and pepper to taste.

Ladle into individual bowls (or side by side with the White Winter Vegetable Soup, as described above). Garnish with green onions and paprika.

WHITE WINTER VEGETABLE SOUP

If you plan to serve these winter vegetable soups together, you can cut the ingredients by half. But bear in mind that both soups freeze very well for up to three months, so it makes sense to make both entire recipes at one time and freeze what you don't use.

Serves 8 to 10

6 TURNIPS, PEELED AND COARSELY CHOPPED

3 PARSNIPS, PEELED AND COARSELY CHOPPED

2 BAKING POTATOES, PEELED AND COARSELY CHOPPED

12 GARLIC CLOVES, PEELED

3 RIBS OF CELERY, COARSELY CHOPPED

2 PEARS, PEELED, CORED, AND COARSELY CHOPPED

10 CUPS CHICKEN STOCK, PREFERABLY HOMEMADE

1 TEASPOON SALT

½ TEASPOON WHITE PEPPER

8 TABLESPOONS (ONE STICK) BUTTER, SOFTENED

½ TEASPOON GROUND GINGER

2 TABLESPOONS FRESH THYME LEAVES

6 GREEN ONIONS, CHOPPED

1 TEASPOON PAPRIKA

Place the turnips, parsnips, potatoes, garlic cloves, celery, and pears in a 5½-quart Dutch oven and cover with chicken stock. Stir in the salt and white pepper. Place over medium-high heat and bring to a boil. Cook until vegetables are very tender, about 25 minutes.

Drain and reserve the stock. Return the cooked vegetables to the pot. Add the butter, ginger, and thyme leaves. Roughly mash vegetables with a potato masher until chunky. Return the stock to the pot and bring to a low simmer. Season with additional salt and white pepper to taste.

Ladle into individual serving bowls (or side by side with the Yellow Winter Vegetable Soup). Garnish with green onions and paprika.

BUTTERNUT SQUASH & APPLE SOUP

*This is one of my favorite soups for brunch parties; I serve it in large mugs so guests can sip while circulating around the room.
If you want a virtually fat-free soup, omit the garnishes of Italian
sausage and Gorgonzola cheese.*

Serves 6 to 8

2 ONIONS, CHOPPED

2 CARROTS, CHOPPED

2 RIBS OF CELERY, THINLY SLICED

2 ROME BEAUTY APPLES, PEELED, CORED, AND CUT INTO
½-INCH DICE

1 LARGE BUTTERNUT SQUASH, PEELED, SEEDED, AND
FIBER REMOVED, CUT INTO ½-INCH DICE

8 CUPS CHICKEN STOCK, PREFERABLY HOMEMADE

SALT AND FRESHLY GROUND BLACK PEPPER

1 TABLESPOON WORCESTERSHIRE SAUCE

8 OUNCES HOT ITALIAN SAUSAGE, CRUMBLED, COOKED
UNTIL BROWN, AND DRAINED (OPTIONAL)

½ CUP CRUMBLED GORGONZOLA CHEESE (OPTIONAL)

¼ CUP CHOPPED FRESH PARSLEY

In a 4½-quart Dutch oven, combine the onions, carrots, celery, apples, and squash. Add the chicken stock and salt and pepper to taste.

Bring to a boil, reduce the heat to a simmer, and cover. Cook for 25 to 30 minutes, or until vegetables are tender.

Strain the solids from the liquid and return the liquid to the pot. Puree the vegetables in a food processor until smooth. Return the pureed vegetables to the pot. Stir in the Worcestershire sauce. Bring just to a boil, then lower the heat. Taste, adding salt and pepper if needed.

Transfer the soup to a tureen or individual bowls and garnish with cooked sausage, Gorgonzola cheese, and parsley.

ROASTED RED PEPPER & BASIL SOUP

*In a pinch, you can substitute canned or jarred roasted peppers for homemade, but fresh basil is an absolute essential.
If you wish, you can omit the cream and Parmesan cheese and
have an almost fat-free soup.*

Serves 6 to 8

8 RED PEPPERS, HALVED AND SEEDED

8 CUPS CHICKEN STOCK, PREFERABLY HOMEMADE

12 LARGE GREEK BLACK OLIVES, RINSED, HALVED, AND PITTED

6 SHALLOTS, FINELY CHOPPED

FRESH HERB BOUQUET OF 1 BAY LEAF, 3 STALKS OF PARSLEY,
2 STALKS OF THYME, AND 1 SPRIG OF ROSEMARY, TIED
WITH KITCHEN TWINE

SALT AND FRESHLY GROUND BLACK PEPPER

½ TEASPOON SUGAR

½ CUP CHOPPED BASIL

1 CUP HEAVY CREAM, WHIPPED TO A SOFT, MOUSSE-LIKE
CONSISTENCY

½ CUP SHREDDED PARMESAN CHEESE

8 SPRIGS OF BASIL

Preheat the broiler. Place the red pepper halves, skin side up, on a foil-lined baking sheet. Place in the oven, about 6 inches from the heat source. Broil until the peppers are charred and blackened, about 10 minutes. Remove from the oven and carefully place the hot peppers in a gallon-sized zip-top freezer bag. Seal the bag and set aside to steam. When peppers are cool enough to handle, slip the blackened skins off and discard.

In a 5½-quart Dutch oven, bring the chicken stock to a boil. Reduce the heat and add the roasted red peppers, black olives, shallots, herb bouquet, and salt and pepper to taste. Simmer for 15 minutes. Strain the solids in a colander, discard the herb bouquet, and return the liquid to the pot. Place the solids in a food processor. Process until smooth, adding a little stock if needed. Return the purée to the stock.

Stir in the sugar, basil, and cream. Bring to just below a boil. Taste, adding more salt and pepper if needed. Ladle into individual bowls and garnish each serving with shredded Parmesan cheese and basil sprigs. Serve at once.

AFRICAN PEANUT SOUP WITH HARISSA SAUCE

Harissa is a fiery hot sauce that is a staple in many Middle Eastern and Northern African dishes, especially couscous dishes. In this recipe, its intense heat is tempered by the silky peanut flavor and the creamy half and half. You can find ready-made harissa in cans or jars at specialty markets.

Serves 8

4 TABLESPOONS BUTTER

2 RED ONIONS, CHOPPED

2 RED PEPPERS, SEEDED AND CHOPPED

2 GARLIC CLOVES, CHOPPED

⅓ CUP FLOUR

10 CUPS CHICKEN STOCK, PREFERABLY HOMEMADE

1½ CUPS CHUNKY PEANUT BUTTER

2 CUPS HALF AND HALF OR MILK

SALT AND FRESHLY GROUND BLACK PEPPER

Harissa Sauce

10 DRIED HOT CHILES, STEMS REMOVED

2 TABLESPOONS CUMIN SEED

2 TABLESPOONS CORIANDER SEED

1 TABLESPOON MUSTARD SEED

2 TEASPOONS CARAWAY SEED

6 GARLIC CLOVES, CHOPPED

½ CUP PACKED CILANTRO LEAVES

⅓ CUP OLIVE OIL

SALT AND FRESHLY GROUND BLACK PEPPER

Melt the butter over medium heat in a heavy 4½-quart Dutch oven. Add the onions, red peppers, and garlic and cook until soft, about 10 minutes. Stir in the flour and cook for 2 minutes. Add the chicken stock and bring to a boil. Whisk in the peanut butter, reduce the heat, cover, and simmer, stirring occasionally, for 15 minutes. Add the half and half or milk, heat gently, and season to taste with salt and pepper.

Serve the soup hot in individual bowls topped with 1 to 2 teaspoonsful of Harissa Sauce.

Harissa Sauce

In a small skillet, break the dried chiles in half and add cumin seed, coriander seed, mustard seed, and caraway seed. Toast over medium-high heat, stirring constantly, until just beginning to smoke and very fragrant. Transfer to a mini food processor and grind until coarse. Add the garlic and cilantro. With the processor running, slowly drizzle in the olive oil and process the mixture into a thick paste. Season to taste with salt and pepper. Harissa Sauce will keep in refrigerator for up to 7 days.

EXOTIC DRIED MUSHROOM & BARLEY SOUP

The savory mushrooms in this soup act as a meat substitute, giving you a soup that is naturally low in fat but high in flavor, with the same rich taste and texture as one made with beef. Experiment with different types of mushrooms. At many supermarkets you can now find such prepackaged blends as Woodland Meadow, Forest Glen, and Wild Bunch.

Serves 8 to 10

1 OUNCE DRIED SHIITAKE MUSHROOMS

1 OUNCE DRIED PORCINI OR OYSTER MUSHROOMS

2 CUPS RED WINE

1 TABLESPOON OLIVE OIL

2 ONIONS, HALVED, PEELED, AND THINLY SLICED

3 CARROTS, THINLY SLICED

4 RIBS OF CELERY, FINELY CHOPPED

1 POUND FRESH BUTTON MUSHROOMS, CLEANED AND THINLY SLICED (SMALLER ONES LEFT WHOLE)

8 CUPS VEGETABLE OR BEEF STOCK, PREFERABLY HOMEMADE

2 TABLESPOONS WORCESTERSHIRE SAUCE

1 (6 OUNCE) CAN TOMATO PASTE

SALT AND FRESHLY GROUND BLACK PEPPER

2 BAY LEAVES, CRUMBLED

1 CUP MEDIUM PEARL BARLEY, RINSED AND DRAINED

1 (10 OUNCE) PACKAGE FROZEN TURNIP GREENS, DEFROSTED

In a large bowl, combine the dried mushrooms and red wine. Let soak for 2 hours. Drain the mushrooms and reserve the wine. Strain the wine through a sieve lined with a double thickness of dampened cheesecloth and set aside. Remove the stems of the mushrooms and discard. Thinly slice the reconstituted mushrooms.

Heat the olive oil in a 5½-quart Dutch oven. Add the onions, carrots, and celery and cook over high heat for about 5 minutes. Stir in the fresh mushrooms and cook until they are just wilted, about 5 minutes. Add the strained red wine, vegetable or beef stock, Worcestershire sauce, tomato paste, salt and pepper to taste, bay leaves, and barley. Bring to a boil, reduce the heat, and simmer, covered, for 20 minutes. Stir occasionally.

Add the reconstituted mushrooms and turnip greens, cover, and continue cooking until the barley is soft, about 15 minutes. Remove the pot from the heat, stir, and taste for seasonings, adding salt and pepper as needed. Serve at once.

HOT CURRIED CREAM OF TOMATO SOUP

Here's a simple way to peel fresh tomatoes: Make an x cut on the blossom ends with a sharp knife. Ladle the tomatoes into boiling water and boil for 15 to 30 seconds. With a slotted spoon, carefully transfer the tomatoes to an iced-water bath to stop the cooking. The skins should slip right off. To seed the tomatoes, cut in half and gently squeeze each half to dislodge the seeds and juice. If you cannot find beautiful vine-ripened tomatoes, substitute with a canned variety.

Serves 8

3 TABLESPOONS OLIVE OIL

1 RED ONION, CHOPPED

4 GARLIC CLOVES, CHOPPED

1½ TO 3 TABLESPOONS CURRY POWDER, PREFERABLY MADRAS

4 TO 5 POUNDS FRESH TOMATOES, PEELED, SEEDED, AND
    COARSELY CHOPPED, OR 2 (28 OUNCE) CANS WHOLE
    TOMATOES WITH THEIR JUICE, CHOPPED

1 CUP BLOODY MARY MIX OR TOMATO JUICE

2 TABLESPOONS FRESH LEMON JUICE

2 TABLESPOONS RED WINE VINEGAR

1 TEASPOON TABASCO

1 TABLESPOON SUGAR

SALT AND FRESHLY GROUND BLACK PEPPER

2 CUPS HEAVY CREAM

1 CUP SOUR CREAM

¼ CUP SNIPPED FRESH CHIVES

In a heavy 5½-quart Dutch oven, heat the olive oil over medium-high heat. Add the onion and garlic and cook, stirring constantly, until the onion just begins to brown, about 5 minutes. Add the curry powder (start with 1½ tablespoons and add more according to your taste) and cook for 3 minutes. Stir in the tomatoes, Bloody Mary mix or tomato juice, lemon juice, red wine vinegar, Tabasco, sugar, and salt and pepper to taste. Cover and cook for 30 minutes, stirring occasionally.

Strain and return liquid to the pot. Puree the solids in a food processor until smooth. Add the pureed mixture back to the pot. (The soup freezes very well at this point. When ready to serve, defrost, heat in a 5½-quart Dutch oven, and continue with the recipe.)

Add the cream and heat until the mixture just begins to simmer. Serve with sour cream and a sprinkling of chives on top.

WHITE CHEDDAR & VEGETABLE SOUP

The sweetness of apple and pear in this soup contrasts nicely with the sharp taste of cheddar cheese. To get a smooth puree, add a little of the stock to the solids when processing. For an extra-smooth texture, press the pureed vegetables through a sieve with the back of a wooden spoon. This rich and creamy soup makes an elegant starter as well as a delicious main course.

Serves 8

2 ONIONS, CHOPPED

3 CARROTS, CHOPPED

2 RIBS OF CELERY, THINLY SLICED

2 SWEET POTATOES, PEELED AND CUT INTO ½-INCH DICE

1 TART APPLE, PEELED, CORED, AND CUT INTO CHUNKS

1 PEAR, PEELED, CORED, AND CUT INTO CHUNKS

10 CUPS CHICKEN STOCK, PREFERABLY HOMEMADE

SALT AND FRESHLY GROUND BLACK PEPPER

2 CUPS MILK

½ CUP HEAVY CREAM

2 TABLESPOONS WORCESTERSHIRE SAUCE

2 CUPS SHREDDED WHITE CHEDDAR CHEESE

8 STRIPS OF BACON, CHOPPED, FRIED UNTIL CRISPY BROWN, AND DRAINED

½ CUP SHREDDED WHITE CHEDDAR CHEESE

½ CUP CHOPPED FRESH PARSLEY

In a 5½-quart Dutch oven, combine the onions, carrots, celery, potatoes, apple, and pear. Add the chicken stock and salt and pepper to taste. Bring to a boil, reduce the heat, cover, and simmer for 25 to 30 minutes, or until vegetables are tender.

Strain and return the liquid to the pot. Puree the solids until smooth in a food processor or blender. Return the pureed vegetables to the pot. Stir in the milk, heavy cream, and Worcestershire sauce. Bring just to a boil, then lower the heat.

Add the shredded cheese, a handful at a time, and whisk until smooth and creamy. Taste and add more salt and pepper if needed. Transfer the soup to a tureen and sprinkle with bacon, additional cheese, and parsley. Serve with slices of toasted, crusty French bread.

BEST BORSCHT

Originating in Poland and Russia, borscht is a wonderful soup that utilizes the much underappreciated beet. Small or medium beets are more tender than large ones. If the beets you buy still have the greens attached, remove them as soon as you get home. The greens tend to draw moisture from the bulbous root. Wear rubber gloves when peeling the beets, as the color can stain your hands.

Serves 8 to 10

10 BEETS

1 RED CABBAGE, HALVED, CORED, AND THINLY SLICED

1 (16 OUNCE) CAN STEWED TOMATOES

2 ONIONS, HALVED, PEELED, AND THINLY SLICED

2 CARROTS, SHREDDED

8 CUPS CHICKEN STOCK, PREFERABLY HOMEMADE

3 CUPS WATER

1 CUP ORANGE JUICE

½ CUP CHOPPED FRESH DILL

¼ CUP BROWN SUGAR

¼ CUP APPLE CIDER VINEGAR

SALT AND FRESHLY GROUND BLACK PEPPER

SOUR CREAM

DILL SPRIGS

Peel and dice 8 of the beets into ½-inch cubes. Peel and grate the remaining 2, using the large holes of a box grater or the medium grating disc of a food processor. Set aside the grated beets.

In a 5½-quart Dutch oven, combine the diced beets, sliced cabbage, tomatoes, onions, carrots, chicken stock, water, and orange juice. Bring to a boil, reduce the heat, and simmer for 45 minutes.

Add the dill, brown sugar, apple cider vinegar, and salt and pepper to taste. Simmer for 10 minutes. Stir in the grated beets and cook for 5 minutes. Adjust seasonings, adding salt, pepper, sugar, or vinegar if needed. The borscht should have a distinctive sweet and sour taste.

Ladle into individual bowls, topping each serving with a dollop of sour cream and a fresh sprig of dill. Serve at once.

WARM & SOOTHING CHUNKY CARIBBEAN GAZPACHO

Most gazpachos are served chilled, but this warmed version is perfect for a winter brunch. I like to place the heated soup in a Crock-Pot, surrounded by various toppings, to keep it warm. If you like, pour a splash of Absolut Peppar or any other pepper-flavored vodka into each serving bowl before filling (or make your own; see page 71).

Serves 8 to 10

1 LARGE ONION, HALVED, PEELED, AND CUT INTO CHUNKS

4 GARLIC CLOVES, PEELED

1 RED PEPPER, SEEDED AND CUT INTO CHUNKS

1 GREEN PEPPER, SEEDED AND CUT INTO CHUNKS

1 CUCUMBER, PEELED, SEEDED, AND CUT INTO CHUNKS

1 (28 OUNCE) CAN WHOLE TOMATOES WITH THEIR JUICE

¼ CUP RED WINE VINEGAR

½ CUP SEASONED BREAD CRUMBS

1½ CUPS BLOODY MARY MIX

1 TEASPOON CELERY SEED

2 TEASPOONS SUGAR

SALT AND FRESHLY GROUND BLACK PEPPER

JERK SEASONING (OPTIONAL)

Garnishes

1 SMALL RED ONION, CHOPPED

1 TOMATO, SEEDED AND FINELY CHOPPED

1 RIB OF CELERY, FINELY CHOPPED

1 RED PEPPER, SEEDED AND FINELY CHOPPED

1 GREEN PEPPER, SEEDED AND FINELY CHOPPED

1 CUCUMBER, SEEDED AND FINELY CHOPPED

6 TO 8 GREEN ONIONS, CHOPPED

2 CUPS LIGHTLY TOASTED, BUTTERED BREAD CUBES

2 CUPS SOUR CREAM

In a food processor or blender, puree the onion, garlic, red and green peppers, and cucumber until finely chopped. Add the tomatoes with their juice, vinegar, and bread crumbs. Process until very smooth. Pour this mixture into a 4½-quart Dutch oven. Bring to a boil, then reduce the heat to a simmer. Cook for 5 minutes.

Stir in the Bloody Mary mix, celery seed, sugar, and salt and pepper to taste. Add the jerk seasoning to taste if desired. Simmer for 3 minutes.

Ladle the soup into bowls. Place the garnishes in individual bowls and pass separately.

ROASTED PEPITA (PUMPKIN SEED) & TOMATO-RICE SOUP

Pepitas are the edible dark green seeds of the pumpkin. When you purchase them, they look different from the seeds you remove when carving a jack-o'-lantern because the whitish outer hulls have been removed. Pepitas have a very delicate flavor and are at their best when roasted and lightly salted. You can find them at many markets today, especially health food stores and those specializing in Mexican cuisine.

Serves 8

3 TABLESPOONS OIL FROM SUN-DRIED TOMATOES (SEE BELOW) OR OLIVE OIL

2 ONIONS, CHOPPED

3 GARLIC CLOVES, CHOPPED

3 RIBS OF CELERY, CHOPPED

2 CARROTS, SHREDDED

1½ CUPS BASMATI RICE

12 SUN-DRIED TOMATOES, PACKED IN OIL, DRAINED AND CHOPPED

1 (28 OUNCE) CAN CHOPPED TOMATOES WITH THEIR JUICE

10 CUPS VEGETABLE STOCK, PREFERABLY HOMEMADE

GRATED ZEST AND JUICE OF 2 LEMONS

⅓ CUP CHOPPED FRESH BASIL

1 CUP ROASTED PEPITAS (PUMPKIN SEEDS)

SALT AND FRESHLY GROUND BLACK PEPPER

1 CUP FRESHLY GRATED PARMESAN CHEESE

In a 5½-quart Dutch oven, heat the oil until hot. Add the onions, garlic, celery, and carrots. Cook over medium-high heat for 10 minutes, or until the vegetables soften. Stir in the basmati rice and cook until the rice begins to puff slightly, about 5 minutes.

Add the sun-dried tomatoes, the chopped tomatoes with their juice, and the vegetable stock. Cover and simmer for 15 minutes. Stir in the lemon zest and juice and basil. Cook for an additional 15 minutes, or until the rice is tender. Stir in the pepitas. Season to taste with salt and pepper.

Ladle into individual bowls and sprinkle some grated Parmesan cheese over each serving. Serve at once.

PUREED LENTIL SOUP

Because lentils need no presoaking time, they are a good alternative to beans for those of us who don't always plan ahead. For an even faster prep time, chop all the vegetables in a food processor, pulsing on and off quickly until you get the desired consistency. Don't splurge and waste your money on the tiny French red lentil. Once cooked, it becomes the same brown color as its common cousin.

Serves 8

1 TEASPOON OLIVE OIL

2 ONIONS, CHOPPED

6 GARLIC CLOVES, CHOPPED

2 RIBS OF CELERY, CHOPPED

3 CARROTS, CHOPPED

1 TABLESPOON CHOPPED FRESH ROSEMARY

2 TABLESPOONS CHOPPED FRESH OREGANO

2 CUPS GREEN OR BROWN LENTILS, WASHED AND PICKED OVER

10 CUPS CHICKEN STOCK, PREFERABLY HOMEMADE

2 BAY LEAVES, CRUMBLED

SALT AND FRESHLY GROUND BLACK PEPPER

JUICE OF 2 LEMONS

1 TABLESPOON GROUND CUMIN

2 CUPS PACKED SPINACH LEAVES, WASHED AND DRAINED, STEMS REMOVED

3 TABLESPOONS CHOPPED FRESH PARSLEY

Garnishes

CHOPPED TOMATOES

CHOPPED GREEN ONIONS

CHOPPED YELLOW PEPPER

STORE-BOUGHT SALAD CROUTONS

Heat the oil over medium heat in a 5½-quart Dutch oven. Add the onions, garlic, celery, carrots, rosemary, and oregano. Cook until the vegetables are wilted and begin to release their own juices, about 10 minutes.

Stir in the lentils, chicken stock, and bay leaves. Bring to a boil, reduce the heat, and simmer for 30 to 40 minutes, or until the lentils are tender. Season to taste with salt and pepper. Stir in the lemon juice and cumin and simmer for 1 minute.

Puree half the soup in a food processor or blender. Return the pureed portion to the pot. Stir in the spinach leaves and remove soup from the heat. When the spinach has wilted, stir in the parsley, taste, and adjust seasonings.

Serve with the garnishes on the side, allowing each person to top his or her soup as desired.

ASPARAGUS & DILL SOUP

Many people consider asparagus a springtime vegetable, but I enjoy this stunning soup year-round. This recipe has been adapted from one in Lee Bailey's Soup Meals. *Lee's method of simmering the asparagus with the stock adds a tremendous amount of flavor to the end result. You can omit the cream, if you are so inclined, since the pureed potatoes add a certain silky texture, but only cream can add that desired lusciousness.*

Serves 6 to 8

2 POUNDS ASPARAGUS, WASHED AND TOUGH ENDS REMOVED

4 TABLESPOONS BUTTER

4 TABLESPOONS CHOPPED FRESH DILL, DIVIDED

1 RED ONION, CHOPPED

2 RIBS OF CELERY, CHOPPED

2 BAKING POTATOES, PEELED AND CUT INTO ½-INCH DICE

8 CUPS CHICKEN STOCK, PREFERABLY HOMEMADE

1 TABLESPOON LEMON JUICE

SALT AND WHITE PEPPER

1 CUP HEAVY CREAM

SOUR CREAM

Snap off the asparagus tips and cut the stalks into 1-inch pieces. In a large nonstick skillet over medium-high heat, melt the butter and stir in 2 tablespoons of chopped dill. Cook for 30 seconds. Add the asparagus tips and sauté for 2 minutes, or until bright green and crisp-tender. Remove the asparagus tips with a slotted spoon and reserve.

Add the red onion, celery, and diced potatoes to the skillet. Cover tightly and cook over very low heat until the vegetables are soft, about 25 to 30 minutes.

Meanwhile, place the chicken stock and asparagus stalks in a 5½-quart Dutch oven. Bring to a boil, reduce the heat, and simmer, covered, for 30 minutes.

With a slotted spoon, transfer the cooked asparagus stalks and the vegetables from the skillet to a food processor. Puree the vegetables, adding a little of the stock to make a smooth, silky mixture. Stir the pureed vegetables into the simmering stock. Add lemon juice, salt and white pepper to taste, and the remaining 2 tablespoons of chopped dill.

Stir in the cream and bring to just below a simmer. Ladle into individual bowls and garnish each serving with a dollop of sour cream and sautéed asparagus tips. Serve at once.

TEX-MEX BLACK BEAN SOUP

The method described here for toasting dried spices comes from Mark Miller of Coyote Cafe fame. The subtle flavor of the spices allows the true taste of the black bean to shine through. As the soup gently simmers, it will naturally thicken, but if you prefer a thicker soup, you can puree up to half the black bean mixture and return this to the pot.

Serves 8

1 TABLESPOON CUMIN SEED

2 TEASPOONS BLACK PEPPERCORNS

1 TEASPOON CORIANDER SEED

1 TEASPOON MUSTARD SEED

2 TABLESPOONS PEANUT OIL

2 ONIONS, CHOPPED

4 GARLIC CLOVES, CHOPPED

2 JALAPEÑO PEPPERS, HALVED, SEEDED, AND CUT INTO
   THIN STRIPS

1 POUND DRIED BLACK BEANS, PRESOAKED (SEE PAGE 9)

1 TABLESPOON CHOPPED FRESH OREGANO

1 TABLESPOON CHOPPED FRESH THYME LEAVES

1 SMOKED HAM HOCK

1 BUNCH CILANTRO, TIED WITH KITCHEN TWINE

2 BAY LEAVES, CRUMBLED

8 CUPS BEEF STOCK, PREFERABLY HOMEMADE

1 CUP TOMATO PUREE

¼ CUP RED WINE VINEGAR

1½ TEASPOONS SALT

JUICE OF 2 LIMES

1 CUP SOUR CREAM

3 TO 4 JALAPEÑO PEPPERS, SLICED CROSSWISE

In a large cast-iron skillet over medium heat, toast the cumin seed, peppercorns, coriander seed, and mustard seed until very aromatic and lightly browned, stirring often to prevent the seeds from burning. This will take about 2 to 3 minutes. Remove from the heat and tie the seeds in a square of cheesecloth. Set aside.

In the same skillet, heat the peanut oil until sizzling. Add the onions, garlic, and jalapeño pepper strips and cook until the onions are translucent, about 5 minutes.

In a 5½-quart Dutch oven, combine the onion mixture, presoaked beans, seeds in cheesecloth, oregano, thyme leaves, ham hock, cilantro bunch, bay leaves, beef stock, tomato puree, red wine vinegar, and salt. Bring to a boil, reduce the heat, and simmer, covered, for 2 to 3 hours, or until the beans are very soft and just starting to fall apart. Add additional water as necessary to keep the beans covered.

Remove the ham hock, cilantro bunch, and the cheesecloth bag and discard. Stir in the lime juice, add more salt and pepper as needed, and serve topped with sour cream and sliced jalapeño peppers.

SAFFRON COUSCOUS SOUP WITH VEGETABLES & DRIED CHERRIES

Saffron is considered to be the world's most expensive spice. Fortunately, a little goes a long way in flavoring and tinting a dish. At grocery stores and farmers markets, it is often kept under lock and key with a sign that says "Ask associate for help."

Serves 8

10 CUPS CHICKEN STOCK, PREFERABLY HOMEMADE

2 TURNIPS, PEELED AND CUT INTO 1-INCH CUBES

1 ACORN SQUASH, PEELED AND CUT INTO 1-INCH CUBES

1 (15½ OUNCE) CAN CHICKPEAS, RINSED AND DRAINED

1 LARGE ZUCCHINI, HALVED LENGTHWISE AND CUT INTO
   1-INCH CHUNKS

2 MEDIUM CARROTS, THICKLY SLICED

2 RIBS OF CELERY, CHOPPED

6 GREEN ONIONS, CHOPPED

1 (16 OUNCE) CAN TOMATO WEDGES WITH THEIR JUICE

1 TEASPOON SAFFRON THREADS

ZEST AND JUICE OF 2 LEMONS

2 CUPS COUSCOUS

1 TEASPOON PAPRIKA

½ TEASPOON GROUND CORIANDER

½ TEASPOON GROUND CINNAMON

¼ TEASPOON CAYENNE PEPPER

1 CUP DRIED CHERRIES

SALT AND FRESHLY GROUND BLACK PEPPER

¼ CUP CHOPPED FRESH CILANTRO

1 CUP CRUMBLED FETA CHEESE

In a 5½-quart Dutch oven, bring the chicken stock to a boil. Add the turnips and acorn squash. Cover and simmer for 20 minutes. Add the chickpeas, zucchini, carrots, celery, green onions, and tomatoes. Cook, uncovered, for 20 minutes, or until the carrots are tender.

In a small bowl, soak the saffron threads with the lemon juice and zest. Let sit for 5 minutes. Stir this mixture into the soup along with the couscous, paprika, coriander, cinnamon, cayenne pepper, dried cherries, and salt and pepper to taste. Cover and simmer for 5 minutes.

Ladle the soup into individual bowls and top each serving with chopped cilantro and feta cheese. Serve at once.

CORN, BLACK BEAN, SERRANO CHILE & JICAMA SOUP

Jicama (pronounced HEE-come-a) is a humble vegetable that hails from Mexico and South America. It has a sweet taste and a delightful crunch, like a curious cross between an apple and a potato. The starchy white flesh lies beneath a fibrous brown skin that has to be completely peeled away. If jicama is not available in your area, substitute 1½ cups of thinly sliced water chestnuts (and change the name of the soup).

Serves 8

3 CUPS FRESH CORN KERNELS (ABOUT 6 EARS)

2 (15½ OUNCE) CANS BLACK BEANS, RINSED AND DRAINED

4 SERRANO CHILES, HALVED, SEEDED, AND VERY THINLY SLICED

1 LARGE JICAMA, PEELED AND CUT INTO ½-INCH DICE

6 CUPS CHICKEN STOCK, PREFERABLY HOMEMADE

2 CUPS MILD SALSA

1 RED ONION, CHOPPED

4 GREEN ONIONS, FINELY CHOPPED

4 GARLIC CLOVES, CHOPPED

1 (4½ OUNCE) CAN MILD GREEN CHILES

1 TABLESPOON CHILI POWDER

1 TABLESPOON GROUND CUMIN

2 TEASPOONS GROUND CORIANDER

SALT AND FRESHLY GROUND BLACK PEPPER

JUICE OF 3 LIMES

½ CUP CHOPPED FRESH CILANTRO

SOUR CREAM

TORTILLA CHIPS

In a 5½-quart Dutch oven over medium-high heat, combine the corn, black beans, serrano chiles, jicama, and chicken stock. Bring to a boil, reduce the heat, and simmer for about 15 minutes, stirring occasionally.

Stir in the salsa, red onion, green onions, garlic, green chiles, chili powder, cumin, coriander, and salt and pepper to taste. Simmer for 10 minutes, or until the vegetables are crisp-tender.

Stir in the lime juice and cilantro. Serve at once, garnishing each bowl with a dollop of sour cream and tortilla chips.

STILTON CHEESE & SCALLION SOUP

Stilton is considered by many to be the king of blue cheeses. Even so, this soup is just as exceptional when made with other members of the blue cheese family, such as Danish Saga Blue, French Roquefort, Italian Gorgonzola, and American Maytag Blue. It is also good made with sharp white cheddar, creamy Camembert, or even a smoked Gouda.

Serves 8

4 TABLESPOONS BUTTER

12 SCALLIONS, THINLY SLICED

1 RED ONION, HALVED, PEELED, AND THINLY SLICED

1 RIB OF CELERY, THINLY SLICED

¼ CUP FLOUR

¼ TEASPOON FRESHLY GRATED NUTMEG

SALT AND FRESHLY GROUND BLACK PEPPER

2 CUPS CHICKEN STOCK, PREFERABLY HOMEMADE

1 (12 OUNCE) BOTTLE OF BEER

5 CUPS MILK

2 CUPS CRUMBLED STILTON CHEESE

1 TABLESPOON WORCESTERSHIRE SAUCE

DASH OF TABASCO

¼ CUP RUBY PORT

1 PEAR, PEELED, CORED, AND VERY THINLY SLICED

¼ CUP SNIPPED FRESH CHIVES

Melt the butter in a 4½-quart Dutch oven. Add the scallions, red onion, and celery. Cook over medium heat until softened, about 8 to 10 minutes. Do not brown.

Sprinkle the sautéed vegetables with flour, nutmeg, and salt and pepper to taste. Cook for 2 minutes. Stir in the chicken stock and beer. Bring the mixture to a boil, cover, and reduce the heat to a simmer. Cook for 15 minutes.

Add the milk and bring the soup just to a boil. Add the cheese in handfuls, stirring each to melt before adding the next handful. Add the Worcestershire sauce and Tabasco. Season to taste with additional salt and pepper if necessary.

Ladle into individual bowls. Top each serving with a drizzle of port, thin slices of pear, and snipped chives. Serve at once with crusty French bread.

SIMPLE ONION SOUP WITH ROQUEFORT & CHIVE TOASTS

This soup is so much easier to eat than the restaurant version! You still get all the taste but will never be socially embarrassed by having a string of cheese stretching between your spoon and the soup bowl. The dark Asian sesame oil and sherry add a rich flavor to these simple ingredients.

Serves 6 to 8

4 TABLESPOONS BUTTER

¼ CUP OLIVE OIL

6 ONIONS, HALVED, PEELED, AND THINLY SLICED

1 TEASPOON SALT

½ TEASPOON BLACK PEPPER

3 TABLESPOONS FLOUR

8 CUPS BEEF STOCK, PREFERABLY HOMEMADE

1 TABLESPOON CHOPPED FRESH ROSEMARY

1 TABLESPOON DARK ASIAN SESAME OIL

¼ CUP DRY SHERRY

Roquefort and Chive Toasts

8 SLICES FRENCH BREAD

¼ CUP CREAM CHEESE, SOFTENED

¼ CUP CRUMBLED ROQUEFORT CHEESE

¼ CUP SNIPPED FRESH CHIVES

In a 4½-quart Dutch oven over medium heat, melt the butter and olive oil. Add the onions and cook for 30 to 45 minutes, stirring frequently. The onions should caramelize and turn a deep, rich brown. Scrape up any browned bits from the bottom of the pan.

Sprinkle the onions with salt, pepper, and flour. Cook for 3 minutes, or until the flour is lightly toasted. Add the beef stock and rosemary. Bring to a boil, reduce the heat, and simmer for 15 minutes. Taste for seasonings and add salt and pepper as needed. Stir in the sesame oil and sherry.

Ladle the hot soup into individual soup bowls and top each soup with a Roquefort and Chive Toast. Enjoy at once.

Roquefort and Chive Toasts

Preheat the oven to 425°F. Place the bread on a baking sheet. In a small bowl, mix together the cream cheese, Roquefort, and chives. Thinly spread the cheese mixture onto the bread slices. Place in the oven and bake for 3 to 5 minutes, or until golden.

SPLENDID SPLIT PEA SOUP

My favorite time to make this soup is right after the holidays, when I put it on the stove to simmer and go about packing up the decorations.
By suppertime, with the house back to normal, I relax and enjoy a warm and soothing bowlful while
reflecting on the memories of the season.

Serves 8

1 POUND DRIED SPLIT PEAS

12 CUPS WATER

1 MEATY HAM BONE (ABOUT 2 POUNDS) OR 2 SMOKED
   HAM HOCKS

2 ONIONS, CHOPPED

4 CARROTS, CHOPPED

2 RIBS OF CELERY, CHOPPED

4 GARLIC CLOVES, CHOPPED

1 TEASPOON SALT

½ TEASPOON BLACK PEPPER

½ CUP CHOPPED FRESH PARSLEY

½ CUP CHOPPED CELERY LEAVES

In a 5½-quart Dutch oven, combine the split peas, water, ham bone or ham hocks, onions, carrots, celery, garlic, salt, and pepper. Bring to a boil, reduce the heat to a simmer, partially cover, and cook for 3 hours, stirring occasionally.

Remove the ham bone and cut away any meat from the bone. Set the meat aside and discard the bone. In a food processor, puree the soup, in batches if necessary, until smooth.

Return the meat and pureed soup to the pot. Stir in the chopped parsley and celery leaves. Reheat, uncovered, for 5 minutes. Serve at once.

BRIE & BROCCOLI SOUP

When choosing a Brie, look for a plump package, a downy-white or cream-colored rind, and a soft, buttery interior. Brie should not have an ammonia smell. I sometimes replace the Brie in this recipe with an equal amount of cream cheese and 1 cup of shredded cheddar cheese.

Serves 6 to 8

2 TABLESPOONS BUTTER

1 ONION, HALVED, PEELED, AND THINLY SLICED

3 GARLIC CLOVES, CHOPPED

2 CUPS SLICED BUTTON MUSHROOMS

FRESHLY GRATED NUTMEG

SALT AND FRESHLY GROUND BLACK PEPPER

3 CUPS BROCCOLI FLORETS (ABOUT 1 HEAD)

6 CUPS CHICKEN STOCK, PREFERABLY HOMEMADE

2 CUPS MILK

8 OUNCES CHILLED BRIE, CUT INTO 1-INCH CUBES, RIND
   INTACT

1 CUP FRESHLY GRATED PARMESAN CHEESE

In a 4½-quart Dutch oven, melt the butter over medium-high heat. Add the onion and garlic and cook for 5 minutes. Stir in the mushrooms and cook until the mushrooms have wilted and most of the liquid has cooked down. Season with freshly grated nutmeg and salt and pepper to taste.

Add the broccoli, chicken stock, and milk. Bring to a boil and reduce the heat to a simmer. Immediately stir in the Brie, a little at a time, and continue stirring until the Brie begins to melt and the soup is thick and creamy. You want to have small bits of unmelted Brie in the soup, so do not let it melt completely.

Season to taste with additional salt and pepper. Stir in half the Parmesan cheese.

Ladle into a soup tureen or individual bowls and sprinkle with the remaining Parmesan cheese. Serve at once.

Note: If the soup sits too long without stirring, it will separate and the broccoli will become limp, so serve as soon as possible.

PAN-ROASTED BARLEY SOUP

Pearl barley, often used in soups and stews, is barley that has had the outer bran removed and then been steamed and polished. It is available in three sizes: coarse, medium, and fine. Pan-roasting the barley adds a deeper flavor to this soup, but if time is of the essence, simply add the barley when you sauté the vegetables.

Serves 6 to 8

3 TABLESPOONS BUTTER

3 TABLESPOONS OLIVE OIL

1½ CUPS MEDIUM PEARL BARLEY, RINSED AND DRAINED

6 SHALLOTS, THINLY SLICED

2 JALAPEÑO PEPPERS, SEEDED AND VERY FINELY CHOPPED

3 CARROTS, SHREDDED

2 CUPS THINLY SLICED BUTTON MUSHROOMS

7 CUPS BEEF STOCK, PREFERABLY HOMEMADE

1 CUP RED WINE

2 TABLESPOONS TOMATO PASTE

SALT AND FRESHLY GROUND BLACK PEPPER

2 TABLESPOONS FRESHLY SQUEEZED LEMON JUICE

6 GREEN ONIONS, CHOPPED

In a 4½-quart Dutch oven over medium heat, melt the butter and olive oil. Add the barley and cook, stirring often, until the barley starts to brown and gives off a nice nutty aroma, about 10 minutes. Do not let the barley burn or the soup will have a scorched taste.

Add the shallots, jalapeño peppers, carrots, and mushrooms. Cook until the mushrooms wilt, about 2 minutes.

Add the beef stock, red wine, tomato paste, and salt and pepper to taste. Bring to a boil, then reduce the heat to a simmer. Cover and cook for about 45 minutes, or until the barley is tender.

Just before serving, stir in the lemon juice and sprinkle the soup with the chopped green onions.

SPEEDY "CREAM" OF BROCCOLI SOUP

This is an ideal soup to make when you are pressured for time. You probably have most of these ingredients on hand already. The addition of mashed potato flakes will thicken the soup quickly and create the velvety texture usually achieved only with fat-laden cream. Best of all, the soup is ready in less than 20 minutes!

Serves 8

3 (10 ounce) packages frozen chopped broccoli, defrosted

1 tablespoon olive oil

2 onions, chopped

¼ cup flour

4 cups milk

3 cups chicken stock, preferably homemade

⅔ cup instant mashed potato flakes

2 to 3 teaspoons herbes de Provence, lightly crushed, or 1 teaspoon poultry seasoning

Freshly grated nutmeg

Salt and freshly ground black pepper

Place the broccoli in a food processor or blender and puree until smooth. Set aside.

Coat a 4½-quart Dutch oven with nonstick cooking spray. Add the olive oil and heat over medium heat. Add the onions and cook until tender, about 6 minutes. Add the flour and cook for 3 minutes, stirring constantly.

Gradually add the milk and chicken stock and continue cooking and stirring until the mixture begins to thicken. Whisk in the potato flakes. Add the herbes de Provence or the poultry seasoning, pureed broccoli, and freshly grated nutmeg, salt, and pepper to taste. Stir until completely heated through, about 8 to 10 minutes. Serve at once.

Hoppin' John is a dish usually served in the South on New Year's Day. I've added Southern greens, another traditional New Year's menu item, to this recipe. The black-eyed peas in the dish are said to represent the fallen Confederate soldiers of the Civil War, while turnip greens eaten on the first day of the year are supposed to bring prosperity for the coming 12 months. With corn bread on the side, a steaming bowlful of this soup in front of you, a spoon in one hand, and the remote control in the other, you're all set for an afternoon of college bowl games.

Serves 8

10 STRIPS OF BACON, COARSELY CHOPPED

1 RED ONION, CHOPPED

4 GARLIC CLOVES, CHOPPED

1 (16 OUNCE) PACKAGE FROZEN BLACK-EYED PEAS

2 (10 OUNCE) PACKAGES FROZEN TURNIP GREENS, DEFROSTED

1 CUP LONG-GRAIN RICE

8 CUPS CHICKEN STOCK, PREFERABLY HOMEMADE

¼ CUP APPLE CIDER VINEGAR

1 TABLESPOON SUGAR

1 (4½ OUNCE) CAN MILD GREEN CHILES

1 (16 OUNCE) CAN TOMATO WEDGES WITH THEIR JUICE

2 JALAPEÑO PEPPERS, SEEDED AND CHOPPED

JUICE OF 1 LEMON

2 TEASPOONS GROUND CUMIN

1 TEASPOON GROUND CORIANDER

SALT AND FRESHLY GROUND BLACK PEPPER

½ CUP CHOPPED FRESH PARSLEY

In a 5½-quart Dutch oven, cook the bacon over medium heat until some of the fat is rendered, about 2 minutes. Add the red onion and garlic. Cook until tender, about 5 to 7 minutes.

Stir in the black-eyed peas, turnip greens, rice, chicken stock, apple cider vinegar, sugar, green chiles, tomatoes, jalapeño peppers, lemon juice, cumin, coriander, and salt and pepper to taste. Bring to a boil, reduce the heat, and simmer, covered, for 25 to 30 minutes, or until the beans and rice are tender.

Stir in the parsley just before serving.

SZECHWAN ASPARAGUS NOODLE SOUP

I like the addition of asparagus to this vegetarian adaptation of hot and sour soup. Be sure not to overcook the asparagus. It offers a wonderful crunch, along with the bean sprouts and water chestnuts. The peanut butter adds a delicately smooth consistency to this fresh and lively dish.

Serves 8

3 GARLIC CLOVES, PEELED

1 TABLESPOON CHOPPED FRESH GINGER

½ CUP SMOOTH PEANUT BUTTER

¼ CUP RICE WINE VINEGAR

¼ CUP LIGHT SOY SAUCE

2 TABLESPOONS DRY SHERRY

2 TABLESPOONS DARK ASIAN SESAME OIL

½ TEASPOON CRUSHED SZECHWAN PEPPERCORNS OR RED PEPPER FLAKES

¼ TEASPOON FIVE-SPICE POWDER (OPTIONAL)

2 TABLESPOONS BROWN SUGAR

8 CUPS VEGETABLE STOCK, PREFERABLY HOMEMADE

12 OUNCES UNCOOKED SPAGHETTI, BROKEN IN HALF

1 POUND ASPARAGUS, CUT ON THE DIAGONAL INTO 1-INCH PIECES

1 CUP BEAN SPROUTS, RINSED AND DRAINED

1 (8 OUNCE) CAN SLICED WATER CHESTNUTS, DRAINED

½ CUP CILANTRO LEAVES

CHINESE CHILE OIL

In a food processor or blender, combine the garlic cloves, ginger, peanut butter, rice wine vinegar, soy sauce, dry sherry, sesame oil, crushed peppercorns or red pepper flakes, five-spice powder, and brown sugar. Process until smooth. Set aside.

In a 5½-quart Dutch oven, bring the vegetable stock to a boil. Add the broken pasta and return to the boil. Cook for 6 to 8 minutes. Add the asparagus and cook for 2 minutes, or until the pasta is firm yet tender (al dente) and the asparagus is crisp-tender. Stir in the contents of the food processor or blender, bean sprouts, water chestnuts, and cilantro leaves. Gently heat for 2 to 3 minutes.

Ladle into individual bowls and drizzle each serving with chile oil.

COLLARD GREEN, PINTO & SWEET POTATO SOUP

Not much prep time goes into making this soulful soup. If desired, ham hocks can be substituted for the turkey drumsticks, but you'll be surprised at the rich, smoky taste the drumsticks provide.

Serves 8

16 OUNCES DRIED PINTO BEANS, PRESOAKED (SEE PAGE 9)

4 ONIONS, HALVED, PEELED, AND THINLY SLICED

4 GARLIC CLOVES, THINLY SLICED

2 SMOKED TURKEY DRUMSTICKS

SALT AND FRESHLY GROUND BLACK PEPPER

1½ POUNDS COLLARD GREENS, WASHED, STEMMED, AND
   CUT INTO 1-INCH PIECES

3 SWEET POTATOES, PEELED AND CUT INTO ½-INCH DICE

½ CUP CHOPPED FRESH PARSLEY

2 TEASPOONS DRIED SAVORY LEAVES

CHEDDAR CORN MINI-MUFFINS (RECIPE FOLLOWS)

PEPPER SAUCE (OPTIONAL)

In a 5½-quart Dutch oven, combine the beans, onions, garlic cloves, smoked turkey drumsticks, and salt and pepper to taste. Add enough water to cover and bring to a boil over medium-high heat. Reduce the heat to low and simmer, partially covered, for about 2 hours.

Remove the drumsticks. Let cool. Add the collard greens to the pot and simmer, covered, for 1 hour. If you want to use the turkey meat, pull the cooled meat from the bones and shred with your fingers. Discard the bones and set the meat aside.

Stir the sweet potatoes, parsley, savory leaves, and optional shredded turkey into the soup. Simmer, uncovered, for 30 minutes, or until the potatoes are tender. It may be necessary to add water if the soup becomes too thick. Taste and adjust seasonings with additional salt and pepper if necessary.

Crumble 2 of the Cheddar Corn Mini-Muffins into each of 8 serving bowls. Ladle the soup over the crumbled muffins and pass the remaining muffins separately. Drizzle with pepper sauce if desired.

CHEDDAR CORN MINI-MUFFINS

I like to make these muffins while the soup simmers. For a lighter muffin, substitute 1 (15½ ounce) can cream-style corn for 2 of the eggs and the corn oil. Reduce the milk to ½ cup. Add 3 tablespoons chopped fresh cilantro and 1 or 2 seeded, chopped jalapeño peppers for a spicy kick.

Makes 36 small muffins

1 CUP ALL-PURPOSE FLOUR

1½ CUPS YELLOW CORNMEAL

1 TABLESPOON BAKING POWDER

1 TEASPOON SALT

1 TABLESPOON SUGAR

2 TEASPOONS POULTRY SEASONING

½ TEASPOON CAYENNE PEPPER

3 EGGS

1 CUP MILK

½ CUP CORN OIL

1½ CUPS FINELY SHREDDED CHEDDAR CHEESE

Preheat the oven to 400°F. Grease and flour 3 mini-muffin tins and set aside. In a large bowl, sift together the flour, cornmeal, baking powder, salt, sugar, poultry seasoning, and cayenne pepper.

In a medium bowl, whisk together the eggs, milk, and corn oil. Make a well in the dry ingredients and pour in the egg-milk mixture. Stir only enough to moisten the ingredients. Add the cheddar cheese. Stir gently until just blended, being careful not to overmix.

Spoon the batter into the prepared tins. Bake for 18 to 20 minutes, or until golden brown. Cool muffins on a wire rack for 5 minutes, then gently remove from the pan. These muffins can be frozen for up to 3 months.

ROASTED CHESTNUT & APPLE SOUP

Fresh chestnuts are available from September through February. To be enjoyed, they must be peeled of their hard outer shell and very bitter inner skin. Canned or jarred chestnuts can be substituted for the fresh ones, thus eliminating the first step in this recipe, but if at all possible, hold out for the fresh variety. Choose nuts that are firm, plump, and without blemishes. The drizzle of pure maple syrup just before serving completes the New England accent of this soup.

Serves 8

2 POUNDS FRESH CHESTNUTS

4 TABLESPOONS BUTTER

6 LEEKS, CLEANED, TRIMMED, AND FINELY CHOPPED

2 GRANNY SMITH APPLES, PEELED, CORED, AND THINLY SLICED

8 CUPS CHICKEN STOCK, PREFERABLY HOMEMADE

SALT AND FRESHLY GROUND BLACK PEPPER

¼ TEASPOON GROUND CINNAMON

¼ TEASPOON CAYENNE PEPPER

1 CUP HEAVY CREAM

3 TABLESPOONS PURE MAPLE SYRUP

FRESHLY GRATED NUTMEG

Preheat the oven to 400°F. Cut an x in the flat end of each chestnut and place on a baking sheet. Roast in the oven for 20 to 25 minutes. When chestnuts are cool enough to handle, peel away the outer skin and inner membrane to reveal the creamy color of the chestnut. If the skins are still difficult to remove after roasting, place the chestnuts in water and parboil them for about 10 minutes, then finish peeling.

In a 4½-quart Dutch oven, melt the butter over medium heat. Add the leeks and apples and cook until the leeks begin to soften, about 3 to 4 minutes. Stir in the chestnuts and quickly sauté for 2 minutes. Do not allow the chestnuts to brown.

Add the chicken stock, salt and pepper to taste, cinnamon, and cayenne pepper. Bring to a boil, cover, and simmer for 45 minutes, or until the chestnuts are very soft.

Strain the soup and return the stock to the pot. Process the solids in a food processor until smooth and creamy. Press the pureed mixture through a sieve or wire strainer to remove any lumps. Return mixture to the pot.

Add the cream and bring just to a boil. Taste and adjust seasonings with additional salt, pepper, and cayenne pepper.

Ladle into individual bowls and drizzle the maple syrup over each serving. Garnish with freshly grated nutmeg and serve at once.

ACKNOWLEDGMENTS

A book is a partnership of many years of experience and the influence of many people. This one is no exception.

Heartfelt thanks to Nathalie Dupree, my mentor, teacher, and friend. Without Nathalie, I would never have discovered my destiny.

To Mara Reid Rogers, my colleague and confidante. Thank you for your constant encouragement and for offering so freely your valuable insights and the benefit of your own literary experiences.

To my assistant, Susan Montgomery, who makes my job a pleasure. And to Mike Montgomery, for his legal savvy.

My admiration and appreciation to all the people at Longstreet Press. To my editor, Suzanne De Galan, quite simply and honestly, you're the best. To Sherry Wade, for her friendly smile and tireless efforts in making copy changes. To Burtch Hunter, for his superb book design. And special thanks to Chuck Perry, Steve Gracie, and Marge McDonald for believing in me, taking a chance, and giving me my first break.

To photographer Mark Hill, and his assistant, Kyle Christy, thanks for your inspired images that make these soups "come to life." Special thanks to my very dear friend Will Deller: As stylist for the book, I appreciate your intricate eye and caring attention to detail. And thanks for always being there for me.

Thank you to the folks at Le Creuset of America and Williams-Sonoma for the many props used in the photographs. Thank you to Lynn Taylor for the use of his unique pottery and to Cam Patton for her lovely bread creations. My appreciation to Donna Faircloth, Jo Anne Rudesill, and Joyce Thompson for lending a hand in preparing the soups for the camera.

Thank you to Jane Fasse, David Duvall, and Sherry Parrish for helping to make the source of these recipes, my cooking school, a success. Thanks to the many apprentices who work behind the scenes, testing and retesting the recipes for my classes and books. And, finally, special thanks to the nearly 10,000 students I have taught over the years. Without your desire to learn and your continued support, none of this would have happened in the first place.

BIBLIOGRAPHY

Bailey, Lee. *Lee Bailey's Soup Meals: Main Event Soups in Year-Round Menus.* New York: Crown Publishing Group, 1989.

Berry, Mary, and Marlena Spieler. *Classic Home Cooking.* London: Dorling-Kindersley, 1995.

Child, Julia. *The Way to Cook.* New York: Knopf, 1989.

Choate, Judith. *The Bean Cookbook.* New York: Simon & Schuster, 1992.

Dupree, Nathalie. *Nathalie Dupree Cooks for Family and Friends.* New York: Morrow, 1991.

_____. *Nathalie Dupree Cooks Great Meals for Busy Days.* New York: Crown Publishing Group, 1994.

Fenzl, Barbara Pool. *Southwest the Beautiful Cookbook.* San Francisco: Collins Publishers, 1994.

Fong-Torres, Shirley. *In the Chinese Kitchen with Shirley Fong-Torres.* Berkeley, Calif.: Pacific View Press, 1993.

The Good Cook. *Soups.* Alexandria, Va.: Time-Life Books, 1979.

Herbst, Sharon Tyler. *Food Lover's Companion.* New York: Barron's Educational Series, 1995.

Hadamuscin, John. *The Holidays: 22 Menus for Elegant Entertaining from Thanksgiving to Twelfth Night.* New York: Crown Publishing Group, 1986.

McGee, Harold. *On Food and Cooking: The Science and Lore of the Kitchen.* New York: Scribners, 1984.

Miller, Mark. *Coyote Cafe: Foods From the Great Southwest.* Berkeley, Calif.: Ten Speed Press, 1990.

Montague, Prosper. *New Larousse Gastronomique.* Twickenham, England: Hamlyn, 1960.

O'Neill, Molly. *New York Cookbook.* New York: Workman Publishing, 1992.

Prudhomme, Paul. *Chef Paul Prudhomme's Louisiana Kitchen.* New York: Morrow, 1984.

Rogers, Mara Reid. *The South the Beautiful Cookbook.* San Francisco: Collins Publishers, 1996.

Sheer, Cynthia. *Soups and Stews: Stocks to One Pot Meals.* Santa Rosa, Calif.: Cole Group, 1995.

Shulman, Martha Rose. *Mediterranean Light.* New York: Bantam Books, 1989.

Southern Living. *The Southern Living Cookbook.* Birmingham, Ala.: Oxmoor House, 1987.

Wells, Patricia. *Trattoria.* New York: Morrow, 1993.

Willan, Anne. *La Varenne Pratique: The Complete Illustrated Cooking Course: Techniques, Ingredients, and Tools of Classic Modern Cuisine.* New York: Crown Publishing Group, 1989.

Wolfert, Paula. *The Cooking of the Eastern Mediterranean.* New York: HarperCollins, 1994.

INDEX

INDEX

INDEX

INDEX